WEST OF IRELAND WALKS

'Clear and lucid and full of enthusiasm, this is
an invitation to don the walking shoes.'
SUNDAY INDEPENDENT

'Excellent – a knowledgeable companion.
If you're heading for the West of Ireland, bring this book along.'
IRISH ECHO

'an invaluable companion … a wonderful introduction
to the living landscape of the West.
User-friendly and accurate.
It's a real find – a book you can use for years.'
TUAM HERALD

Kevin Corcoran has an intimate knowledge and love of the Irish landscape. An environmental biologist, he has studied the West of Ireland both professionally and as a rambler, and lectures on Ecology and Environmental Studies. Operating a private nature reserve, he is tirelessly involved in the repair and creation of natural habitats, for both educational and preservation purposes.

Conscious of the constant degradation of the natural environment, he is a keen supporter of the Irish Wildlife Federation and their efforts to purchase and preserve diminishing habitats. An ardent advocate of sustainable living with the natural environment, he presently lives as an Eco-dweller and rejects all forms of mass consumerism. Much of his free time is spent hill walking, sketching, writing and recording the demise of our natural environment.

About WEST CORK WALKS and KERRY WALKS

'If you have a wondering eye, a wandering pair of legs,
and a yen to visit two of the most beautiful counties …
don't neglect to pack a Corcoran … Dipping into
KERRY WALKS and WEST CORK WALKS is as refreshing
as taking a draught from a mountain stream.'
BELFAST TELEGRAPH

KERRY WALKS

'… expert understanding of the Irish countryside,
its flora and fauna.'
Dan Collins, THE EXAMINER

WEST CORK WALKS

'… an expert and informative book …
Kevin Corcoran is a dab hand at drawing, whether plant
or landscapes or his carefully explicit maps.'
Michael Viney, THE IRISH TIMES

West of Ireland Walks

Text and illustrations
Kevin Corcoran

THE O'BRIEN PRESS
DUBLIN

This revised edition first published 2012.
First published 1993 by The O'Brien Press Ltd,
12 Terenure Road East, Rathgar, Dublin 6, Ireland.
Reprinted 1997. Revised 2000. Revised 2004. Revised 2008.

ISBN 978-1-84717-287-7

British Library Cataloguing-in-Publication Data
A catalogue record for this title is available from The British Library

6   7   8   9   10   11
12   13   14   15

Cover photograph by Kevin Corcoran
Typesetting, editing, layout, design: The O'Brien Press Ltd
Printed and bound by CPI Group (UK) Ltd, Croydon, CR0 4YY
The paper used in this book is produced using pulp from managed forests

The walks in this book have been designed to ensure comfortable access to the countryside
with due consideration to landowners. Rights-of-way were followed and sought where
possible; however, the fact that a walk is outlined in this book does not necessarily
guarantee a recognised right of way.

Land ownership and conditions can change, and where such problems do arise the author
would appreciate such changes being brought to his attention so that future editions can be
modified. The author and the publishers do not accept any responsibility where trespass
may occur, neither do they accept any responsibility for accident or loss by the public when
carrying out these walks. Commonsense should prevail at all times. Take the advice of locals
and heed all warning signs. On no account should dogs be taken on any of these walks as
they cause annoyance and disturbance to livestock, wildlife and to members of the public.
Show respect for the countryside – the irresponsible actions of one person can destroy the
enjoyment of so many others.

Contents

Dedication:
To all those who love and respect Nature

INTRODUCTION

Wild, windswept, rain-lashed and wave-torn, on first acquaintance the west of Ireland seems cold and desolate. However, frequent exposure to this raw country does not repel, but compels one to explore its almost infinite tracts of rugged wilderness in greater detail. Endless plains of bog roll across abandoned moors, towering peaks poke rumbling cloud-filled skies, high cliff-edged glens hide mirror lakes, while white-foamed waterfalls and cascades plunge from the lofty watch-towers of mountain summits. Waves of pounding surf erode the tattered coastline of deep fjords and island-cluttered bays, while stretches of golden sands and folds of shattered rock rebuke the frenzied Atlantic. The magic of Ireland's wild west is haunting and unreal.

These varied and exposed conditions contain many wild inhabitants. The turbulent seas are home to important colonies of marine birds and mammals, the watery bogs and moors hold significantly rare species of plants, strange flowers from other climates grow in rich profusion about the rocky hills and mountain slopes, while the coastal heaths retain delicate and threatened wildlife occupants. Such a landscape is not only romantically charming but is a shining jewel in a world that is becoming increasingly polluted. The west of Ireland is very much an untouched landscape that seems far removed from the rush of modern-day life.

But how safe is this wilderness? What does the future hold for our threatened and diminishing wild places? The pressure on society to maintain economic growth and meet the needs of an expanding population will continue to exert a destructive force on the environment. Clearly a more balanced approach is required, one that takes stock not only of ecological requirements but also of the needs of economic growth. All too often a unique habitat or landscape falls victim to commercial exploitation, whether it be forestry, mining, urban and recreational development, tourism or agriculture, while simple environmental aesthetics fade quickly before the immediacy of jobs and economic progress.

Fortunately a greater awareness has begun to develop and now more and more people see the need for a better understanding of and respect for our countryside. Ireland's uniquely clean landscape is becoming an attraction as an area to explore.

MINIMUM IMPACT

Pollution, tourist pressure, litter, habitat destruction, wildlife disturbance and extinction are all having a serious impact on the outdoors. How then do we take seriously our need to preserve the diminishing natural environment at a time when more and more people want to experience it? How do we reconcile our presence in it at the same time as we try to protect it from us?

Obviously there is a need for a strong set of guidelines which will ensure that the effect of the rambler on the environment is one of minimum impact. There is one very basic guideline: leave the countryside as you yourself would like to encounter it.

Rubbish – whatever its source – is objectionable and we should all help to remove any non-biodegradable litter – plastic, aluminium foil wrap, cans and bottles.

Interfering with populations of wild plants and animals is also irresponsible as many have a limited distribution and are already under threat from diminishing habitats. This is their home. We are mere visitors and should act accordingly.

Many of the wild places are touched by and even part of someone else's workplace, especially the farming community. Therefore we should always respect and appreciate both their privacy and their rights and in no way interfere with their property or cause damage to it. The best rule for walkers is: become part of the solution not the problem.

These walks have been designed to introduce the walker to our wild and perilously threatened heritage in as safe a manner as possible. They have been categorised into three levels according to their degree of difficulty and the level of fitness required. There is no more miserable way of spending a day than taking on something that is beyond your limits or that you are not suitably equipped to cope with. So check the walk's suitability for your party before setting out. Then you will ensure a good day is had by all.

Casual: These are fairly straightforward walks following well-defined paths and roads. They are suitable for first-time and occasional walkers with young children. None of the more expensive and varied equipment used by regular walkers, such as compasses, waterproof boots and all-weather coats, is necessary. However sensible clothing is required.

Moderate: These walks cover a certain amount of rough terrain with more taxing conditions such as steep or wet ground. Therefore they are more suited to those who have already engaged in some amount of walking. You need to be reasonably fit, wear waterproof boots with a good grip and appropriate clothing.

Tough: These walks are really for the more experienced walkers who have a lot of mileage under their belt. They include a lot of very tough terrain that does not always follow an outlined path. Thus you need to be very fit and experienced at coping with awkward conditions. Additionally you need to carry a compass, have strong waterproof boots and all-weather clothing, be able to read maps carefully and accurately and to work out a certain amount of facts for yourself in relation to finding your way.

THE WALKS

Walking through the various habitats that are found in Ireland's west, one comes to know the occupants of these diminishing communities, of their fragile existence and the forces that now threaten them. From woods, mountain, bog, beach, cliff, dune, to freshwater lake and river, all are visited at different seasons of the year and their significance illustrated and explained. I have no doubt that they will draw you out again and again to experience the delights of an ever-changing landscape throughout the seasons. However, it is not realistic to assume that there will be no danger involved just because these areas have been outlined in the book. It is important to remember a number of points listed below.

DANGER

Commonsense and discretion should always be used in the wilderness, especially if you are not familiar with the ways of the countryside. Please take note of the following points.

Mountains: The higher peaks are prone to rapidly descending fogs and mists which make it impossible to descend safely, so attempt these only on fine clear days when there is no threat of rain and its accompanying low cloud. Do not enter the high mountains on your own.

Cliffs: These should be treated with the greatest of respect, especially in wet and windy weather when they can be prone to erosion and instant collapse. During wild, windy weather, strong gusts of wind can blow you from the cliff-top. Thus visit them during suitable weather only and keep your distance from the edge. On no account allow children free reign near them.

Waves: Freak waves may thunder on to the shore during stormy and windy weather. These can turn up irregularly every fifteen to twenty-five minutes, depending on the swell. Most people like to get near the crashing waves on a headland or a rock, measuring their safety distance by the waves immediately observed. Tragically, many lives have been lost over the years as unwary visitors have been caught by a sudden enormous freak wave.

Rights-of-way: As far as was possible all the routes in this book follow recognised rights of way, are across commonages or have been given the blessing of the owner. But in some cases it was not possible to discern this fully – or the land may undergo a change of ownership. In general, most landowners are reasonable as long as you respect their property and they are treated with the courtesy they deserve. If difficulties do arise, please be discreet and leave the property promptly but safely. The author would appreciate any such instances being brought to his attention so that future editions of this book can be modified.

Dogs: These should never be brought into wilderness areas where sheep farming is an important part of people's livelihood. The very smell of a strange dog affects sheep, causing them to panic. Unfortunately many walks have now been closed off to the public because of the arrogance and selfishness of some dog owners.

Clothing: Wear good boots that have a reasonably good grip. Wet and cold weather can occur at any time of the year, thus you should dress accordingly. It is better to wear several layers of warm clothing than one thick garment as layers can be taken off and put on depending on conditions. For this purpose it is handy to have some form of knapsack that leaves your hands free. On the tougher walks a spare pair of shoes and socks is desirable.

USING THE BOOK

Ideally the text should be read in conjunction with the walk, but it is a good idea to read the entire walk before you set out. Each walk follows a series of numbered points on the accompanying map, with the text at each point providing directions and outlining what to see. Use the map regularly to check your location. Starting at point (1) follow the dotted line on to point (2), and so on throughout the route. Note that the end of some walks overlaps the outward route and thus the numbered points reappear in the text. If you should lose your bearings at any time try to find your position on the map and refer to the numbered point immediately before it in the text. This should explain your next move.

WALK DESCRIPTIONS AND CHARACTERISTICS

Distances: All are given for the round trip with the extra distance for the OPTIONS given separately.

Time: This is given as an approximate minimum for the completion of the round trip. Obviously this will vary greatly according to the type of walker. On average give yourself half-an-hour per mile on the casual walks but an hour per mile for the tough ones, adding on as much time as you like for rests, picnics and so on. In winter be careful of the early sunset and the inevitable darkness which can occur from 16.30pm onwards – SET OUT EARLY!

WALKS SUMMARY

WALK	HABITAT	LENGTH	TIME	SUITABILITY

THE BURREN

WALK	HABITAT	LENGTH	TIME	SUITABILITY
1 Sliabh Eilbhe	green roads	6ml/9.6km	3–3.5hrs	casual
2 Black Head	limestone uplands	9ml/14.5km	4.5–5hrs	tough
3 Abbey Hill	green roads and limestone hill	4ml/6.5km	2–2.5hrs	moderate

COUNTY GALWAY

WALK	HABITAT	LENGTH	TIME	SUITABILITY
4 Inishmore	Aran island	11.2ml/18km	5–5.5hrs	moderate
5 Mount Gable	upland bog	4ml/6.5km	3.5hrs	moderate
6 Errisbeg Mountain	Coastal mountain	3ml/5km	3hrs	tough
7 Maumturk Mountains	upland peaks	9.5ml/15km	7hrs	very tough
8 Lackavrea Hill	upland heath	5ml/8km	4–5hrs	moderate
9 Killary Harbour	sea fjord	6ml/9.6km	3hrs	moderate

COUNTY MAYO

WALK	HABITAT	LENGTH	TIME	SUITABILITY
10 Cong	woodlands	5.5ml/9km (OPTION 0.5ml/0.8km)	3hrs (OPTION 0.5hrs)	casual
11 Lough Nadirkmore	mountain lake	6ml/10km	4–5hrs	tough
12 Tonakeera Point	beach	5ml/8km	3.5–4hrs	casual
13 Croagh Patrick	wooded countryside	9ml/14.5km	5hrs	casual
14 Achill Head	cliff tops	4.5ml/7km	4–4.5hrs	moderate

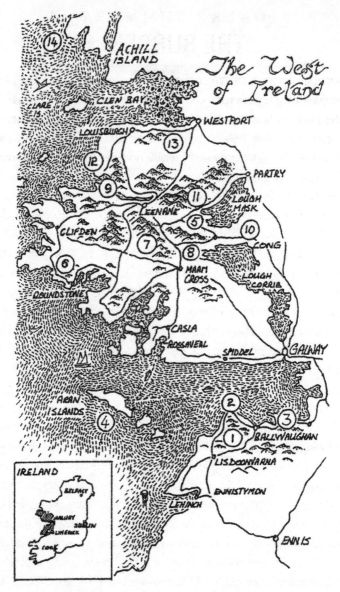

1. Sliabh Eilbhe; 2. Black Head; 3. Abbey Hill; 4. Inishmore; 5. Mount Gable;
6. Errisbeg Mountain; 7. Maumturk Mountains; 8. Lackavrea Hill;
9. Killary Harbour; 10. Cong; 11. Lough Nadirkmore; 12. Tonakeera Point;
13. Croagh Patrick; 14. Achill Head.

THE BURREN

THE STRANGE TRACT OF WILDERNESS known as the Burren is one of the most fascinating regions to be encountered anywhere on the western edge of the Eurasian landmass. This is a barren bleached terrain of shattered limestone rock that runs in serried sheets and terraced layers across abandoned hills and silent valleys, where no gurgling streams, no dense woods nor lush green pastures grace the folds of its bony skeleton-like emptiness. The Burren was formed from the countless shells of marine animals, which were deposited at the bottom of the sea many millions of years ago, and the resulting sedimented limestone was later pushed up above the waves to produce this strange landscape. Now seventy million years later, the area stands tattered and worn by the driving winds and corrosive rains that blow in from the nearby wild Atlantic. As limestone is a soft, easily dissolved rock, erosion has scarred and pitted it with numerous cracks and crevices through which the ground water quickly vanishes into a maze of subterranean rivers, that give the land the appearance of an arid desert.

On closer inspection the Burren's strangeness becomes even more astounding as here among the lifeless rocks is a most fascinating collection of flora. Wondrous Arctic, Alpine and Mediterranean plants thrive, acid-loving side-by-side with the alkaline, and woodland species growing in this treeless terrain. This is a phenomenon as bizarre as discovering seaweed and cacti growing on a dry, cold mountain-top, and increases the feeling that this land is of another world, far removed from the shores of Ireland. Such is the eerie fascination of the Burren that makes it one of the most captivating wonderlands to be explored anywhere on the island of Ireland.

NOTE: Three different walks are outlined for the Burren, one tough (Black Head), one moderate (Abbey Hill) and one casual (Sliabh Eilbhe). As a result there is some repetition of several points in each walk to cater for the different levels of walker. A full explanation of the Burren's characteristics is included in the Black Head walk.

1 – Sliabh Eilbhe

WALK DESCRIPTION

LOCATION: From the village of Ballyvaughan travel west around Black Head for 7ml/11km until Fanore is reached. Take the first LEFT turn-off up the Caher valley and continue for another 2ml/3.2km to a Y-junction. At the junction go to the RIGHT and after a few hundred metres watch for the rough open space on your RIGHT which has a sign for 'Black Head Loop + Caher Valley Loop'. Only a limited amount of parking is available here, so please park with some consideration for others.

TERRAIN: This is a casual walk along a circular route that is ideal for both young and old. The route throughout is well defined as it follows the delightful green roads around the high hill of Sliabh Eilbhe and

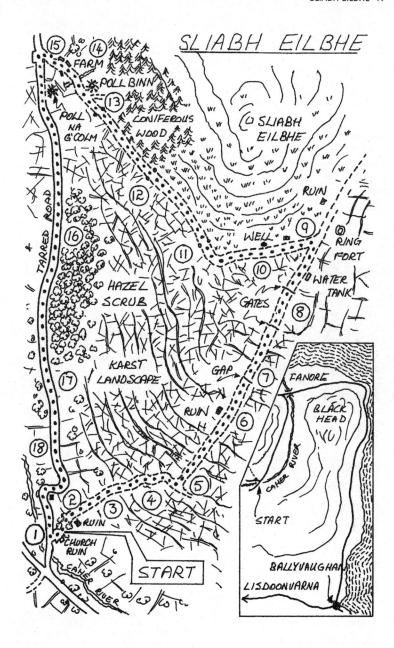

SLIABH EILBHE

returns along a quiet, tarred byroad that runs through some excellent stretches of limestone karst landscape.

FEATURES: Old green roads; karst landscape; unique Burren flora and fauna; caves, swallow-holes and underground rivers; heather-clad moors; holy well; ring forts and ruined church.

LENGTH: 6ml/9.6km.

TIME: 3–3.5 hours.

EQUIPMENT: Comfortable water/muckproof walking boots are necessary as there are a few muddy patches along the green roads; runners or ordinary shoes would be less than ideal. Wear suitable clothing during wet or windy weather. OS map No. 51.

WHEN TO WALK: Perfect at any time of the year as long as you are suitably dressed.

The harebell's delightful lilac-coloured blooms may be seen all over the Burren in late summer.

WALK OUTLINE

(1) The entrance to the old green road is at the top of the grassy lay-by. This is partially obscured by thickets of BLACKTHORN (*Prunus spinosa*) bushes through which the track passes in tunnel-like fashion.

(2) Very soon the track opens out again and passes by some abandoned stone cottages. From here on, high stone walls guard the route as it gradually climbs the hill.

These old tracks criss-cross the rocky wilderness of the Burren and are the ancient routes of the former inhabitants of the region. Though rough underfoot, they were once the main routes of commerce for cattle and humans and were never intended for heavy vehicles. Fortunately a large number of the routes still survive and provide the basis for the extensive Burren Way walking route as well as providing the rambler with access to the wild countryside.

(3) As you walk along this idyllic green road, crowded thickets of colourful wild flowers greet the eye during the summer months. Many of these blossoms are the reason for the Burren's fascinating uniqueness, coming as they do from the extreme corners of mainland Europe.

Large numbers of the flowers encountered are true residents of the mineral-impoverished calcareous habitat. The HAREBELL (*Campanula rotundifolia*) has dancing, bell-shaped lilac-coloured flowers that contrast sharply with the grey limestone walls, while the BLOODY CRANE'S-BILL (*Geranium sanguineum*), with its blood-red blossoms, glows from dark rock crevices. But it is the presence of odd plants like the yellow-flowered NORTHERN BEDSTRAW (*Galium boreale*), the white-flowered IRISH EYEBRIGHT (*Euphrasia salisburgensis*) and the blue-petalled SPRING GENTIAN (*Gentiana verna*) that leaves one puzzled, as these plants are more suited to the colder climes of the Arctic and the high Alps. It is thought that they may well be remnant species from glacial times which still manage to survive on the barren and exposed habitat that the Burren offers.

(4) Higher up, the characteristic karst landscape of the Burren becomes increasingly prevalent.

Looking over the wall on your right, you see the flat and fractured pavements of bare

The mother shipton moth may be spotted amidst the blossoms of mountain avens.

limestone run across the hillside, the many-fissured crevices hiding a multitude of unique and rare flowers. In the early summer months these miniature sunken gardens produce their most spectacular display. With a bit of searching you will discover the HOARY ROCK-ROSE (*Helianthemum canum*), MAIDENHAIR FERN (*Adiantum capillus-veneris*) and the DENSE-FLOWERED ORCHID (*Neotinea maculata*), all very characteristic of Mediterranean regions. Although both the Arctic-Alpine and the Mediterranean plants are quite common in their respective habitats, the fact that they are found together only in the Burren makes this one of the strangest and most important carboniferous limestone regions in western Europe.

(5) Nearer the hilltop and at a bend in the road, a rough Y-junction is reached with a yellow arrow marker. Take the LEFT fork, following the direction of the arrow and ignore the smaller track branching off to the right.

Throughout the summer you will surely encounter some of the many butterflies and moths that inhabit this flower-filled paradise. Early in the season the first to emerge from their winter hibernation are the commoner varieties of butterfly like the ORANGE-TIP (*Anthocharis cardamines*) and the SMALL TORTOISESHELL (*Aglais urticae*), both of which can be seen flitting about the coloured blooms. Later on in the season rare butterflies like the PEARL-BORDERED FRITILLARY (*Clossiana euphrosyne*) and the BROWN HAIRSTREAK (*Thecla betulae*) may be found. Two rare moths, the BURREN GREEN (*Calamia tridens occidentalis*) and the TRANSPARENT BURNET (*Zygaena purporalis*), are rarely found outside the Burren's limestone borders.

(6) At the top of the hill, the road levels out and you pass some stone ruins on the left.

There are some fine views here over the surrounding hills, with the terraced slopes of Gleninagh Mountain behind you, the heath-clad hill of Sliabh Eilbhe up ahead and panoramic glimpses of the Aran islands out to sea on your right. Looking across the heath on your right, sheets of the white-flowering MOUNTAIN AVENS (*Dryas octopetala*) stretch as far as the eye can see. This is another of the unique Alpine plants so characteristic of this limestone wilderness and it grows here with great vigour right down to sea level. The flowers appear at their best in June and July and are replaced by long, feathery seed heads in autumn. Strangely enough, the mountain aven is actually a shrub, not an herbaceous flower, as is easily recognised by its tough and creeping woody stems. If you are in luck you may spot the unusual MOTHER SHIPTON MOTH (*Euclidimera mi*) which tends to visit the flowers of the mountain avens. The moth has a strange pattern on its wings that looks like the outline of an old woman.

(7) Presently a gate is reached that crosses the track. This has a stile on its right for easy passage. Please use the stile rather than climb over the gate.

Now that the path is bordered by lower walls you can get on to the vegetation-cloaked limestone more easily. Be extremely careful of the many cracks and crevices that lie hidden beneath the thin layer of heath as a slip can bring painful consequences.

(8) Later on, pass by another three iron barred gates using the adjacent stiles. Please keep the gates closed as cattle or sheep often graze these apparently barren hills.

The presence of livestock atop the higher Burren hills in winter is another interesting indicator of the region's uniqueness. Normally in winter, cattle are taken down to the lowlands, but in the Burren the reverse is more the norm. This is due to the fact that limestone tends to store heat, as a consequence grass keeps on growing throughout the winter months, providing essential feeding during this leaner time of the year. Such a phenomenon in no small way plays its part in allowing the many strange occupants of the Burren to survive in a wilderness that at first sight appears to be totally hostile to their existence.

(9) Eventually, you pass a large concrete water tank inside the wall on your right, after which you reach the third gate with a stepped stile on its left-hand side. Passing through the stile the green road begins to descend the hill and passes a walking pole marker.

You must now keep alert for another track, without walls, that branches off to the LEFT. This is a good 200m further on and crosses over the heath towards the left-hand side of Sliabh Eilbhe. About here, the outline of a circular stone ringfort can be seen down on the hill to your right. If you pass a roofless but well-preserved stone ruin on your left you have missed the turn-off by a few metres.

The fort down to the right appears as nothing more than a circular enclosed field and it is one of a very large number of such structures scattered across the length and breadth of the Burren. Not in any way as complex or impressive as the large stone fort of Cathair Dhúin Irghuis on Black Head, these much simpler structures are possibly of a later origin, some as late as the fifth century AD, and were used as dwellings for a single family. A simple timber-framed house stood within and a high fence around the perimeter protected livestock from wolves.

(10) Following the LEFT turn-off, pass through an iron barred gate by opening and reclosing. The muddier, grass covered track now maintains a STRAIGHT course around the side of Sliabh Eilbhe mountain.

Soon you will notice a conspicuous black-and-white cross atop a metal-enclosed concrete pillar on your right. This is the site of a holy well known as Tobar an Athair Calbhach (the well of Fr Calbhach). Near the cross is a well with a number of stone steps leading down to its crystalline waters; a clutter of religious objects and offerings decorate the surrounding stone cracks. As it is still used as a place of devotion, please do not disturb those who may be here to pray, and grant them the respect they deserve.

If here after rain, you will soon realise that this is no ordinary well but an opening to an underground stream which courses its way through the subterranean caves that riddle the porous limestone of the Burren, making it like Swiss cheese. If there has been ample rain then a torrent of water will be flowing through the well as it follows its subterranean course. However, after drought the water may be very still or even non-existent. There are very few overground rivers found within the karst landscape. Over the millennia most have eaten their way into the easily dissolved limestone to create a most spectacular series of underground rivers and caves, many of which are explored by pot-holing enthusiasts. Beneath Sliabh Eilbhe runs the longest cave system known in Ireland, a distance of 7.5ml/12km. Further on during the walk, we will pass close to its chilling and precipitous entrance, Poll na gColm (Colm's Hole), from which point the many experienced pot-holers descend into the geological heart of the Burren.

(11) With the well behind you, follow the lane as it swings around to the right and heads towards a forestry plantation. Keep on the green road, passing through all gates by opening and reclosing them or using the adjacent stiles. DO NOT climb over the gates.

Across the limestone terrain on your left and up along the heather-clad slopes of Sliabh Eilbhe on the right, the contrast in the vegetation is unmistakable. Here, stretched out before you, is a classic example of the geological extremes occurring on the Burren. On the left are the typical karst features of the area, primarily exposed and porous limestone through which water quickly percolates giving a dry, arid landscape with its associated flora. On the right, a large layer of shale covers Sliabh Eilbhe's limestone heart. This prevents the rainwater from draining downwards, instead causing it to accumulate in the soil to create a totally different habitat of wet heath and blanket bog. And so, as you walk, the left-hand verge throws out the alkaline-loving Alpines such as MOUNTAIN AVENS (*Dryas octopetala*), SPRING GENTIANS (*Gentiana verna*) and FRAGRANT ORCHIDS (*Gymnadenia conopsea densiflora*), while on your right, waves of acid-loving HEATHERS (*Erica*), HEATH-SPOTTED ORCHIDS (*Dactylorhiza maculata*) and MOUNTAIN EVERLASTING (*Antennaria dioica*) run up the side of the hill.

(12) The dank sterility of the SITKA SPRUCE (*Pinacea sithensis*) forest skirts the track on the right, supporting very little of the native species of wildlife. Looking down to the left is a much more rewarding scene in the upper reaches of the Caher river valley with its thickets of hazel scrub and more open meadows.

The pine marten is a rare and very distinctive mammal, but hard
to spot because of its secretive nature.

If here in early May and June, keep your ears open for the numerous
CUCKOOS (*Cuculus canorus*) that occupy the Burren during their short
visit to Ireland from their winter quarters in Africa. A rich insect
population and an ample supply of safe nesting sites ensure large
numbers of MEADOW PIPITS (*Anthus pratensis*) and, as a consequence,
large numbers of cuckoos breed in the locality. The meadow pipit is
one of the main bird species that the female cuckoo lives off, laying her
egg in the pipit's nest and allowing the poor deluded pipit to raise the
voracious youngster at the expense of her own brood.

Nature, though often cruel, is wonderfully balanced and the number
of meadow pipits and cuckoos would normally never vary. That is until
Homo sapiens casts its cold-blooded shadow across the wilderness.
Now the number of pipits and, as a consequence, the number of
cuckoos, is decreasing due to their loss of habitat. Sadly the cuckoo
looks destined to follow the same fate as the CORNCRAKE (*Crex crex*)
and disappear altogether. It will be a sad day when the haunting call of
the spring cuckoo across the awakening countryside is no more.

(13) Halfway through the coniferous plantation and near a rough track
on your right, you may be able to see a small circular enclosure of stones
and wire, although it is gradually being enclosed by further planting.

This is Poll Binn, a dangerous swallow-hole that leads down to the caverns below and into which a small stream that has just escaped from the soggy slopes of Sliabh Eilbhe vanishes. Many of the Burren's rivers disappear as soon as they are formed, and rarely get a chance to flow across the limestone.

Down across the meadows to your left is the enormous swallow-hole entrance to Poll na gColm. (The best access to this is from the tarred road ahead after point 15. This is on private land and admission to it is at the discretion of the owner.) If you do decide to visit Poll na gColm, please remember that it is extremely dangerous and can be accessed safely only with the help of ropes. Even then it can be disquieting as, after rain, a river pours over the side of the swallow-hole, crashing down in a thunderous roar to the underground passages. The possibility of the caverns filling with water after an unexpected downpour is a real prospect and enough to keep me, at least, well away from this sport!

Therefore it cannot be over-emphasised that entering these dangerous caverns is completely outside the scope of amateurs, who should confine themselves instead to Aillwee Cave where they can be led safely beneath the hills by experienced guides.

(14) Shortly beyond Poll Binn, a third gate, with a stile on the left side, leads into a farmyard. Pass through the stile and follow the track past the farm buildings down on to the tarred road.

Just before you enter the farmyard another stream flows from Sliabh Eilbhe, passes underneath the track and then vanishes down a natural crack in the limestone. This small swallow-hole is very obvious on your left.

(15) Pass through the imposing pillars of the farm entrance, turn to the LEFT and follow the tarred road down the hill. A little way down, a break in the wall allows easy access to Poll na gColm, if you wish to visit it.

On the right-hand pillar of the farm's gates is an inscription carved on a limestone slab. This is a little hard to make out but it relates to the famine relief work that was carried out in this region in 1848, when many of the roads were banked up and the bordering stone fences built.

(16) As the quiet country road leads you downwards, the barren limestone pavement returns.

However, the left-hand side of the road carries a dense thicket of short stunted HAZEL (*Corylus avellana*) scrub. This is the typical habitat of the Burren's most beautiful inhabitant, the PINE MARTEN (*Martes martes*). A shy wary creature, it keeps well clear of us humans, thus it is unlikely that you will spot it. Still, the pine marten lives quite successfully in the Burren, one of the few habitats in Ireland where it survives. It is a rich, chocolate-brown colour and has a long bushy tail, and is a large mammal related to the BADGER (*Meles meles*). As it feeds not only on small birds but also upon animals like rats and mice, the pine marten plays an important role in the countryside helping to keep some species in check.

(17) Access to the karst landscape now becomes possible where the old stone walls have crumbled. In the many creviced grykes between the pavement clints, you can get a good look at the vegetation that survives in the sheltered environs; these are mostly Arctic-Alpine plants with some woodland types like IVY (*Hedera helix*) and HART'S-TONGUE FERN (*Phyllitis scolopendrium*). And here and there you will see delightful clumps of acid-loving heathers growing directly on top of the alkaline limestone. Nothing can explain this phenomenon satisfactorily. This magic, however, is part of the Burren's enigma.

(18) Further down, the tree cover and more fertile farmland increase. This is due to the coating of glacial drift upon the valley floor which also explains why the nearby Caher river is one of the few rivers in the Burren to flow above ground from source to sea.

(1) Beyond the scattering of houses at the bottom of the valley lies the car park and the end of the walk.

Hidden beneath the bushes on the right as you enter the lay-by are the remains of an old church. This is Formoyle Church, which was in use up until 1870, but is now in ruins.

2 – Black Head

WALK DESCRIPTION

LOCATION: The walk starts near the church of St Patrick on the western coastline of Black Head. Travel west along the coast road from Ballyvaughan for 7ml/11.2km until the dunes and caravan park of Fanore are reached. Take the first LEFT turn by the bridge over the Caher river, with a sign for St. Patrick's Church. Beyond the church, find a suitable, wide road margin to park sensibly, as the church yard is now locked to prevent people from using it. Failing this, the only other practical way to find parking is to drive a further kilometre on the main road and park in the public car park at Fanore beach. You must then walk 1km along the main road to reach the green road and the walk's start. Not the most ideal during the peak tourist season.

BLACKHEAD

CATHAIR AN
AIRD ROIS

19
20
GATE
21

STONE
WALLS

18

17

16

15

DEEP
HOLLOW

14

GLENINAGH MOUNTAIN

13 DOBHACH
    BHRAININ

12

11

CATHAIR DUIN
IRGHUIS

10

9   8   7

WALLS

6

5

4   3

23

KHYBER
PASS

START

ST. PATRICKS
CHURCH

1

2

22

CAHER RIVER

BALLYVAUGHAN

START

BLACK
HEAD

FANORE

TERRAIN: A tough circular walk that in part follows the outline of the delightful green roads but also crosses the scarred and pitted limestone pavements on the ridge of Gleninagh Mountain. The ground underfoot is dry but the shattered and fissured rock is difficult and uncomfortable and at times dangerous. Thus you need to be extremely fit and agile, capable of skipping over the many cracks and crevices, and able to manage a steep ascent (1045ft/320m). Several stone walls also have to climbed.

FEATURES: Limestone karst region; rare plants; botanical curiosities; unusual insect and animal life; Bronze Age forts; panoramic views of Burren landscape and Galway Bay; glacial features; one of the Burren's few overground rivers.

LENGTH: 9ml/14.5km.

TIME: 4.5–5 hours.

EQUIPMENT: Strong, comfortable walking shoes with a reliable and good grip. A wind- and rain-proof jacket for the exposed high plateau of Gleninagh Mountain. A knapsack to carry additional clothing, and refreshments for at least one stop. A comfortable pair of casual shoes for the two miles of tarred road at the end of the walk. OS map No. 51.

WHEN TO WALK: Suitable at any time of the year when the weather is favourable and there is no risk of fog or low cloud engulfing the higher hills. The most rewarding time to explore is May or June, when many beautiful and unusual flowers are on display. But there is a rich profusion of colourful plants in flower throughout the summer and the autumn.

WALK OUTLINE

(1) Having parked near the church, walk back down to the T-junction with the main road and go to the right.

In front of you, expansive dunes hide a golden beach, both very much out of place amid the rocky wilderness of this stony coast and not representative of the type of terrain that is to be discovered ahead. However, such close proximity to the sea does play a crucial role in the Burren's uniqueness. These rough Atlantic waters experience the effect of the North Atlantic Drift, a warm current that wells up from the Equator and prevents any extreme temperature drop during the winter months. As a consequence, severe winter frosts and snow are practically unknown in this region.

(2) At the T-junction go to the RIGHT, walking very carefully along the busier road for about 200 metres until you reach a lane between several modern houses, on the RIGHT. This has a sign for Fanore Cottages.

(3) On reaching the lane follow it up to the RIGHT and proceed gradually uphill until you meet a sharp right-hand bend, next to another modern bungalow.

In July and August thick clumps of purple-flowered HAREBELL (*Campanula rotundifolia*) grow from the old walls. In Ireland, this plant is generally confined to the west and grows with great profusion in the Burren. Behind the walls, the rough meadows are richly adorned with the blossoms of summer's growth, with many common species spilling out on to the laneside, such as OX EYE DAISY (*Chrysanthemum leucanthemum*), COMMON KNAPWEED (*Centaurea nigra*), LORDS-AND-LADIES (*Arum maculatum*) and HEDGE BINDWEED (*Calystegia sepium*). The rocky mineral-impoverished soil is able to support a greater concentration and range of wild flowers than more fertile meadows. Paradoxically, it is because of the Burren's infertility that the many rare plants can survive.

(4) On arriving at the sharp bend by a well kept bungalow, continue STRAIGHT on by using the stile in the stone wall to exit from the laneway and onto the 'green road' at the other side. Follow the green road STRAIGHT across the open field to reach an iron barred gate, with an adjacent stile, at the other side. Passing through this second stile leads onto the better sections of green road. Some cattle may be in the field so be sure to reclose the gate after you.

The china-blue petals of the spring gentian are on full display in April and June.

The HAWTHORN (*Crataegus monogyna*) and BLACKTHORN (*Prunus spinosa*) bushes growing here are severely pruned and shaped by the wind that blows in off the Atlantic coast. Trees are rare in the Burren due to the lack of soil, to coastal exposure, and to erosion by both the weather and grazing animals. However, there is some indication that the area did contain a certain degree of tree cover in former times, though it is unlikely that it would ever have been extensively forested, as the many rare plant species to be encountered would not have survived the suffocating forest canopy.

(5) Another gate and a number of stone walls will cross the green road. Please close the gate and climb the stone walls carefully at their strongest points by the corners and replace firmly any stones you may dislodge.

The old walls that run along the side of the track are made from the fractured remains of the surrounding limestone. Built without earth or mortar, they are quite stable and have stood for a long time as the open spaces between the stones allow the strong gale-force winds to pass easily through without causing damage. Looking at the stones carefully, you may be lucky enough to discover some of the fossilised remains of shells embedded in them, giving a very clear indication as to the origins of the limestone rock.

(6) Two more stone walls have to be crossed as the green road gradually rises up towards the horizon ahead. The terrain of

grey-bleached limestone rock runs up the terraced hills on the right and you can also get glimpses of it running down to the coast and out under the waves. However, nearer the lane the fissured limestone is covered in a thin blanket of soil that gives rise to small meadows.

Throughout the spring and summer months these meadows are crowded with a most impressive collection of wild flowers. Many are quite common, others are exceedingly rare and seem out of place, while some, such as the increasingly rare COWSLIP (*Primula veris*), are disappearing due to loss of habitat. However, it is the curious presence of strange plants like IRISH EYEBRIGHT (*Euphrasia salisburgensis*), SPRING GENTIAN (*Gentiana verna*) and MOUNTAIN AVEN (*Dryas octopetala*) that add an interesting puzzle to the tale. These three are all Arctic-Alpine plants that normally thrive atop high mountains and in the snow-covered lands of the frozen north. So how is it that they are growing here so far south and by the sea? To make matters even more confusing, a little searching will introduce you to the DENSE FLOWERED ORCHID (*Neotinea maculata*) and the VERNAL SANDWORT (*Minuartia verna*), growing alongside the Arctic-Alpine plants. These plants are also out of place as they normally grow in the hot dry Mediterranean. So again one wonders how they are able to survive so far north in this cool damp climate! Indeed, this is a very puzzling landscape where plants from opposite extremes of Europe can happily co-exist. This strange mix of northern and southern plants is one of the more fascinating features of the Burren and an occurrence not found anywhere else in western Europe.

(7) When the lane swings around a bend there are good views across the mouth of Galway Bay. Far out to sea are the Aran islands, an extension of the Burren limestone and with equally impressive karst features and an associated collection of unusual plants. As you look straight across the bay, the coastal sprawl of Spiddal is apparent, running as it does all the way into the inner reaches of Galway city. Beyond Spiddal, the high peaks of the Twelve Bens and Maumturk mountains poke from the desolate landscape of Connemara's spell-binding wilderness, their

quartzite peaks glistening in showery sunshine.

(8) Presently, another wall crosses the track and a low cliff on your RIGHT leads you up towards the brow of Black Head.

Here the low thorny stems of the delicate BURNET ROSE (*Rosa pimpinellifolia*) bloom throughout the summer months, thriving in its preferred habitat of dry coastal heath. A rose of a different nature also thrives in the dry limestone, HOARY ROCK-ROSE (*Helianthemum canum*). This extremely rare shrub, with its yellow flowers, is another of the unusual Mediterranean plants that is quite happy to live here in one of its only Irish locations outside the Aran islands.

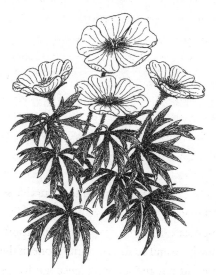

In late summer the bright red blossoms of the bloody cranes-bill may be seen poking from the many limestone crevices.

You may wonder if all these strange plants were introduced by humans! This is unlikely as the pollen analysis of the bogs shows us that these plants have been around for a long time, long before humans ever set foot on this island.

(9) Having reached the brow of the hill, leave the laneway and begin the ascent up the barren limestone hill on your RIGHT to arrive at a ruined stone fort.

As you climb, the extent of the bare limestone becomes increasingly apparent. Approximately three hundred and forty million years ago, during the Carboniferous Period, this whole area sank beneath the sea where it remained for all of eighty million years. During this time the skeletons of numerous marine creatures rained down upon the seabed, building up a limestone deposit to a depth of almost a thousand metres. This, in time, rose above the sea and became covered in sedimentary silts of mud before it sank for a second time and another layer of sedimentary limestone developed. Finally, the seabed re-emerged about seventy million years ago to be scoured by the action of wind, rain and numerous ice ages to leave us the fractured and barren landscape that we now see around us.

(10) On arriving at the fort of Cathair Dhúin Irghuis (the fort of Irghuis) maintain a STRAIGHT line past the fort and head for the steep terraces ahead.

Located on a strategic and prominent look-out point, this circular stone fort possibly dates from the Bronze Age over four thousand years ago. It must surely have been used for defensive purposes with its commanding views of the surrounding coastline and Galway Bay. During this time, wave after wave of migrating tribes arrived to stake their claim on Ireland. The history of these peoples is lost to us as no written records of their deeds survive, only the complex and faint strands that have been handed down to us through mythology with its mix of fable, magic and half-truths. And so we have the sketchy stories of the warrior-like Firbolgs who are believed to have built many of the great forts like Dún Aonghasa on the Aran islands and possibly Cathair Dhúin Irghuis. Then came the magical Tuatha Dé Danann who are thought to have erected many of the ancient burial tombs and court cairns, but mythology has reduced their race to fairy folk who live beneath the hills and forts. Finally, came the Milesians who in time gave rise to the social structure that was still in existence with the arrival of Christianity in the fifth century AD.

It is also believed that some of the stone walls surrounding Dhúin Irghuis are part of the original layout of the fort, so please treat them with respect if you have to climb over them. Sadly, the fort is disintegrating with time – and the tendency of visitors to clamber indifferently over the loose stone walls is not helping to preserve the structure. If this continues, it will surely become just another heap of stones and the ancient history hidden within its shadows will recede even further.

(11) Beyond the fort, a stone wall is encountered. Cross this carefully and proceed towards the cliff directly ahead.

Walking across the flat pavements of rock and jumping over the crevices one finds a great emptiness with little colour other than the grey expanse of fretted limestone. The smooth floor-like slabs are known as clints, while the separating clefts are called grykes and are characteristic of karst regions. Running in parallel lines across the hills, these grykes initially developed as cracks. With time, rain and frost widened them into the deep chasms they are today, some expanded until they almost join, with only a thin, knife-edge ridge in between.

Surface vegetation is notably absent and you wander through a seemingly dead landscape of sterile rock. However, the observant explorer quickly notices another of the Burren's astonishing features, for here beneath your feet is probably the biggest rock garden in all of Europe. Hiding in the sunken hollows like miniature herbariums is a multitude of rare plants, seldom found outside the Burren. Throughout the summer months you find the MAIDENHAIR FERN (*Adiantum capillus-veneris*), BLOODY CRANE'S-BILL *(Geranium sanguineum)*, DARK-RED HELLEBORINE (*Epipactis atrorubens*), and SHRUBBY CINQUEFOIL (*Potentilla fruticosa*), as well as the SPRING GENTIAN (*Gentiana verna*), MOUNTAIN AVEN (*Dryas octopetala*) and an incredible collection of orchids. Little wonder that the Burren has become internationally recognised as the most important Carboniferous limestone region in western Europe.

(12) On reaching the first of the low cliffs, climb up where possible, crossing over two walls, and then maintain a STRAIGHT course across the series of terraces until the top of Dobhach Bhrainín is reached. In all, about five low cliffs have to be scaled before you arrive at the final terrace where the summit is marked by a low cairn of stones.

The cliffed terraces occur where sedimentary layers of silt are sandwiched between layers of limestone. This silt eroded more quickly than the limestone, causing the then overhanging limestone to crumble and ultimately form a demarcating cliff.

As you walk you see an occasional blanket of vegetation covering the limestone pavement, especially at the cliff bases. A lot of this is due to the fact that wherever a layer of silt lies at the base of a cliff, the subterranean springs cannot penetrate it and so the water emerges to provide welcome moisture for the plants. Still, this does not explain why the drier parts of the Burren can support such an interesting collection of wild flowers. Several factors are now known to work hand-in-hand to produce this unusual situation.

Many of the Mediterranean plants prefer dry conditions and in theory should not grow in the wet soggy climate of Ireland. But the heavy rainfall quickly drains through the limestone to maintain relatively dry conditions. Additionally, during drought the porous nature of the rock can draw up water from the subterranean rivers like a sponge and maintain sufficient moisture for the well-being of the plants.

Limestone can store heat and the grykes provide adequate shelter from the wind. Thus miniature regions of mild climate exist within the many hollows.

With time, sufficient soil has built up within the grykes for plants to take root and grow. The soil is severely lacking in essential nutrients, but this has been a blessing for the rarer Arctic-Alpine plants. These plants thrive in the impoverished confines of high mountains or in freezing climates with their montane characteristics of rocky, barren, exposed, mineral-deficient soil and an absence of competition. Limestone, though lacking in minerals, is alkaline and provides a beautiful crumbly soil within which great numbers of bacteria thrive. The bacteria extract minerals like nitrogen from the air in sufficiently low quantities to prevent the development of quick-growing, high-nutrient-demanding grasses, but enough to support the slower-growing, hardy flowering plants. If the soil was mineral-rich, the grasses would thrive, blocking out all light from the grykes and smothering the slower-growing plants. So the lack of competition due to the barrenness of the region has proved to be an act of providence for the rarer species.

Thus a combination of limestone's porosity, dryness, sheltered grykes, alkaline nature and infertility, the absence of competition, exposed position and finally, the influence of the warming North Atlantic Drift have all contributed to making the Burren the unique paradise it is.

(13) Having reached Dobhach Bhrainín (1036ft/314m), the first of Gleninagh Mountain's twin peaks, continue STRAIGHT on to the second peak marked by a long flat-topped mound. This will involve curving slightly to the LEFT to descend on to a low saddle and then climbing up another series of stepped cliffs to gain the opposite summit.

The top of Dobhach Bhrainín is marked by a small cairn of stones and there are excellent views to be had over the sea into Galway city, across to Connemara and over the Burren countryside stretching south to the Cliffs of Moher. You may also encounter some of the herds of wild goats that are found wandering about these hills – it is not unusual to detect their smell long before you see them! They are thought to have originated from the domesticated stock of the ancient tribes of Ireland. Having successfully returned to the wild state, they now play an important part in maintaining the ecological balance of the region. Diligent grazers, they help to prevent the spread of suffocating scrub like the low-growing HAZEL (*Corylus avellana*), which if left unchecked would greatly reduce the extent of the rarer wild flowers. As soon as any of the invasive hazel shrubs germinate and grow up above the grykes, they are quickly pruned back by the ravenous goats.

(14) Descending on to the saddle, an enormous depression or hole is discernible to the right. Avoid climbing down into this as its steep sides are difficult to scale. Maintain a STRAIGHT course along the top of the saddle, working your way CAREFULLY across the deeply fissured limestone towards the cliffs of the next summit ahead.

Here the barren limestone pavement is at its most spectacular. As one looks about this moonscape, those often-quoted words attributed to one of the officers in the army of the seventeenth-century conqueror, Oliver Cromwell, seem very apt: 'The Burren yields neither water enough to drown a man, wood enough to hang a man nor soil enough to bury a man.'

The large depression on the right is possibly due to the collapse of part of the massive network of caves and underground caverns that riddle the limestone, and into which all the rivers, springs and streams have vanished through swallow-holes. So much a feature of the easily eroded limestone, these underground caves are a delight to the pot-holing enthusiast, with some extending for several miles and many more running out under the sea floor.

(15) On reaching the second summit (1046ft/317m) with its long flat-topped grassy mound and concrete pillar, turn ninety degrees to the RIGHT and head for the next rise, visible in the distance across the heather-clad plateau. Please note that one needs to exercise a considerable degree of caution when crossing this plateau as a thin covering of vegetation hides the many cracks and crevices of the underlying limestone.

From the top there are good views down to fertile green fields that run out to the shoreline of reddish seaweed-spattered rock. A close scrutiny of the shoreline will reveal the profile of Gleninagh Castle, a fine sixteenth-century tower house of one of the region's principal ruling Gaelic families at that time, the O'Loughlinn's.

(16) Crossing the plateau, stay in the centre and avoid descending the sloped sides of the adjacent valleys.

Up here a heathland-type vegetation dominates, with SEDGES (*Carex*), prostrate JUNIPER bushes (*Juniperus communis*), HEATHER (*Erica*) and in the wetter callows, swards of the yellow-flowering BOG ASPHODEL (*Narthecium ossifragum*) being quite common. All these plants are generally acid-loving and more usual on bogs and wet heaths. Their survival is possible wherever a substantial amount of debris has built up on the limestone to keep the roots of these plants from making contact with the more alkaline nature of the rock.

Slow worms amidst the maidenhair ferns, a sight unique to the Burren.

You may also spot the numerous snails that inhabit these quarters as the limitless supply of calcium-rich limestone is perfect for the construction of their shells. Several dozen different species occur in the Burren but many of these are not easily seen on the exposed karst terrain as they stay within the deep grykes feeding on the varied vegetation. However, up here they can be seen foraging on the accessible surface vegetation and after rain their numbers can be quite spectacular. Some are rather large like the BLACK-LIPPED HEDGE-SNAIL (*Capaea nemoralis*). This has a conspicuous lip around the mouth of the shell, while the banded shell itself can vary in colour from brown to yellow. At the other extreme is the tiny CHRYSALIS SNAIL (*Vertigo species*), all of two millimetres in length.

The many slugs (without a shell) and snails (with a shell) provide food for another stunning occupant of the Burren which, if encountered, can give quite a shock as it looks exactly like a snake! Its sinuous, scaly and legless body, which can be up to 1ft/30cm long, winds its way in and about the vegetation and over the rocks. With its tongue darting in and out, it has all the features of the fearsome reptilian creature. However, it is in fact a lizard that has lost its legs through evolutionary adaptation. This is the SLOW WORM (*Anguis fragilis*), a harmless reptile that is a native of mainland Europe and was probably introduced into Ireland in the recent past. Although the Burren holds a great collection of strange species, there are no records of this animal having ever existed in the wilds of Ireland prior to the 1960s. Unfortunately, introducing non-native species usually has serious repercussions for the native residents. For example, one need only mention the devastating effect of the imported plant, rhododendron, on our native forests in Killarney and the effect the American mink is having on our river life after it was recklessly released from fur farms in the 1950s.

(17) On reaching the next grassy mound go at an angle to the LEFT towards a stone wall. Cross the wall and continue walking at right angles to the wall across the grassy heath.

(18) Presently the grass gives way once again to the barren limestone, which runs off into the distance along the flat mountain ridge. Maintain a STRAIGHT course along this plateau, crossing as many as six walls. The last one brings you out on to a green road.

As you walk, many of the by now familiar flowers of the Burren will be met, but there are still quite a considerable number of rarities to be discovered. One particularly fascinating group is that of the many rare and beautiful orchids of the region. In all, there are as many as twenty-seven different types of orchid found throughout Ireland and of these over three-quarters are to be found in the Burren. The orchids are the BEE, FLY, BUTTERFLY, BIRD'S-NEST, FROG, FRAGRANT, PYRAMIDAL, SPOTTED and PURPLE, TWAYBLADE, DARK-RED HELLEBORINE, and, my own favourite, the rare and fragile AUTUMN LADY'S TRESSE. As well as their fascinating flower shapes, the delicate and vulnerable life cycles of the orchids are very interesting. Many orchids take a considerable length of time to develop their photosynthesising leaves, during which time they are dependent on symbiotic fungi to nourish them. Some orchids take as many as fifteen years to develop the flowers and seeds which ensure their survival through to a new generation. Thus picking any of them can have dire consequences for their survival as a species, especially when their range is already reduced to a critically narrow level and they are very close to extinction. In many cases, extinction occurs because of the work of the selfish and naive collector; such is the case with the rare MAIDENHAIR FERN (*Adiantum capillus-veneris*), which has been greatly decimated by plant collectors invading the Burren.

(19) On reaching the green road go to the RIGHT and continue downhill into the Caher valley. This track is part of the Burren Way.

At the hilltop near some pillars, the remains of the ancient stone fort Cathair an Aird Rois (fort of the high door) are easily accessible on your left, another of the vast number of ancient dwelling sites found throughout the Burren. Even though they were in all likelihood used as defensive dwelling structures by the original builders, later civilisations used them for a multitude of other purposes, a circumstance which makes it difficult to ascribe a date to their origins.

This fort continued to be used up until recent times and the remains of a chapel and shebeen are visible within its walls. The shebeen was an illegal drinking house where much merriment and dancing occurred during religious gatherings.

(20) As you descend, the fertile farmland returns, its green meadows full of wild flowers throughout the summer months. Where the water accumulates in soggy corners, the sweet smell of MEADOWSWEET (*Filipendula ulmaria*) wafts through the air come the month of August. Due to glacial deposits, a layer of silt covers the limestone of the valley floor allowing a more productive land to develop. It is presumably around such land that the greater concentration of ancient dwellings was, for obvious reasons, located. Across the meadows to your right, but not visible, is another fort and the ruins of a deserted village or

what some people believe to be a *clachán*, an ancient settlement of the serf class that existed within the old Gaelic system, which could be several hundred years old.

(21) On reaching the tarred road go to the RIGHT, passing another junction that almost immediately branches off to the left.

A greater concentration of hazel scrub skirts the roadside, providing a gentle change from the bare landscape just explored. The very low concentration of trees in the Burren means bird life is notably reduced, with a severe shortage of the common passerines or songbirds. However, where there is adequate cover provided, as here in the Caher valley, the FINCHES, ROBINS, THRUSHES and BLACKBIRDS provide a welcome sound during the spring and early summer months. Because of the area's frost-free climate, even during severe winters, great flocks of these small birds are not uncommon and in some cases hundreds of CHAFFINCHES can be encountered as they scour the hedgerows for food. Many of these migrate to the Burren from the colder interior of the midlands.

(22) After a mile or so the road crosses a bridge over the Caher river. This is the only large Burren river that flows overground for its total length of four miles, a most unusual occurrence. This river is also the home of an extremely rare PONDWEED known only by its Latin name (*Potamogeton perpygmaeus*), a hybrid of the fen pondweed and lesser pondweed.

(23) Shortly before the walks end the road runs through what is known locally as the Khyber Pass. On the left it is bordered by steep rocky slopes while on the right the river has eaten into the soft banks of silt that cover the valley floor, clearly illustrating the nature of the material that allows the river to remain above ground.

(1) Presently, the sea comes into view again and you arrive back at St Patrick's church and the walk's end.

3 - Abbey Hill

WALK DESCRIPTION

LOCATION: The walk starts at the church of St Patrick, 7ml/11km from Kinvara or 5ml/8km from Ballyvaughan on the Ballyvaughan-Kinvara road. There is ample parking space in the church car park.

TERRAIN: A moderate circular walk that follows a stretch of green road and also crosses the limestone terraces of Abbey Hill. You need to be fit and agile as the limestone slopes are rough underfoot with many cracks and crevices. The descent down from the top of Abbey Hill is tough with a number of stepped ledges to be negotiated. Therefore it

ABBEY HILL

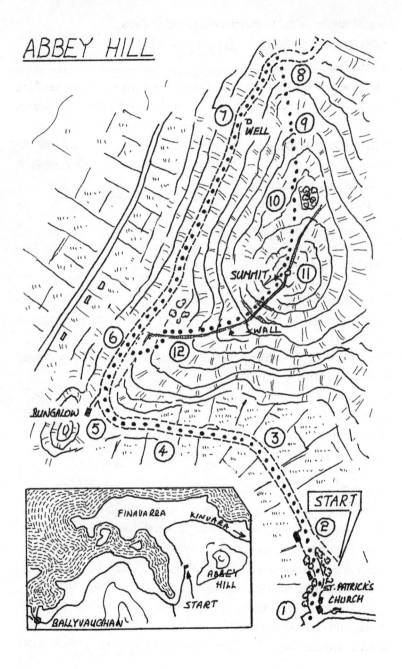

would not be suited to inexperienced hill walkers.

LENGTH: 4ml/6.5km.

TIME: 2–2.5 hours.

FEATURES: Karst, limestone landscape and green roads; unique flora and rare species; panoramic views over Galway Bay and the Burren hills; views of twelfth-century Corcomroe Abbey; holy well.

EQUIPMENT: Walking boots with a good grip are necessary for the bare limestone pavement as this can become quite slippery after rain. A walking cane is desirable.

WHEN TO WALK: Suitable at any time of the year.

WALK OUTLINE

(1) Having parked in the large open space by the church, locate and follow the narrow tarred road that goes up beside the church and past the rectory.

The road is overhung with tall SYCAMORE trees (*Acer pseudoplatanus*) and leads up to a number of houses and a farmyard. The sycamore tree is not a native of Ireland's ancient forests and in no way reflects the type of forest canopy that must have existed in these parts in former times. There is much argument as to whether the Burren was ever fully forested. A certain amount of pollen analysis shows

In winter, large flocks of redwing thrushes may be seen flying over the wet meadows.

that trees, especially pine, did occur more frequently than they do now and the suggestion has been made that forest clearance and subsequent over-grazing caused the complete erosion of the soil to leave the bare limestone landscape we see today. However, such erosion would have been widespread and certain areas, like this more fertile valley and the high heather-clad slopes of Sliabh Eilbhe, would surely not have escaped. It is more probable that forests did exist in localised pockets and that the barren limestone of the higher plateaus is a permanent feature exposed by the cleansing effect of the last Ice Age.

(2) Presently you pass the last of the houses on the left and the road reverts to a stony track. Maintain a STRAIGHT course.

Green fields skirt the old road on either side, presenting a very different picture of the Burren. But the higher slopes of Abbey Hill up to the right are reminders of the limestone landscape that still dominates this north-eastern corner of the Burren. Being very close to the shoreline of Galway Bay with its numerous mud flats, large flocks of wader birds, such as CURLEW (*Numenius arquata*) and LAPWING (*Vanellus vanellus*), probe the soft ground throughout the winter months. You should also spot loose flocks of migrant thrushes, such as the FIELDFARE (*Turdus pilaris*) and REDWING (*Turdus iliacus*), combing the fields in search of grubs and worms. Where hawthorn trees are plentiful, these birds will strip them of their rich bounty of red berries. During the summer the farmed fields present little to look at, the track verges providing more variety with BRAMBLE (*Rubus*) and DOG ROSE (*Rosa canina*) clambering up through the few bushes. These two straggling plants are in flower from July onwards and are regularly visited by nectar-seeking butterflies like the SPECKLED WOOD (*Pararge aegeria*).

(3) The green road swings around to the LEFT and there are good views down over the neighbouring Poll na gCloch Bay (the hole of the stones) which is well shielded from the more open sea of Ballyvaughan Bay by the small peninsula of Finavarra.

For a relaxed and very casual walk, Finavarra is a delightful area to explore. Numerous seals populate the bay and you can spot both the GREY SEAL (*Halichoerus grypus*) and the COMMON SEAL (*Phoca vitulina*). On the northern, seaward side of the peninsula is the curious flaggy shore, a delightful stretch of limestone rockpools full of the spiney SEA URCHIN (*Echinus esculentus*). The neighbouring and shallow coastal waters hold colourful molluscs, crustaceans and, of course, the famous Galway Bay OYSTERS. As a consequence, University College Galway has a marine research station at the adjacent Loch Muir, a land-locked sea lake.

However, such a rich bounty also attracts the undesirable who exploit the environment for their own ends. Visiting fishermen, for example, in one week stripped the entire foreshore of every single sea urchin, eleven tons in all, an act that depleted the population and greatly reduced the area's unique wildlife potential. If properly protected, this potential could greatly enhance the area's appeal to the new generation of environmentally conscious visitors now being attracted to Ireland. It is to be hoped that in time the marine community will return to its former glory.

Near the flaggy shore stands Mount Vernon lodge, the one-time holiday home of the early twentieth-century socialite Lady Gregory. Here, she entertained many well-known Irish novelists such as WB Yeats, George Bernard Shaw, Oliver St John Gogarty and JM Synge.

(4) The road continues to climb with little change in the surrounding landscape. But keep your eyes open for the many different types of flower that can be discovered along the track. As well as the plentiful supply of plants like the HAREBELL (*Campanula rotundifolia*), COMMON KNAPWEED (*Centaurea nigra*) and SHEEP'S BIT (*Jasione montana*), you should also find less common varieties like the GRASS OF PARNASSUS (*Parnassia palustris*), a white flowering plant, not a grass, that is rarely found growing in the southern part of the country.

(5) On reaching the top of the hill the road swings around to the RIGHT and you pass a bungalow on the left.

Cuckoo bumblebees will be found about the pink flower-heads of knapweed.

From here on the green road levels out and there are excellent views down over the green meadows of the Dooras peninsula and out across Galway Bay towards the city. Dooras is another interesting coastal strip with extensive tidal mud-flats and inlets. Many birds frequent the area in winter, especially migrants such as BRENT GEESE (*Branta bernicla*), WIGEON (*Anas penelope*) and WHOOPER SWAN (*Cygnus cygnus*). During the summer, native species dominate, such as the long-legged GREY HERON (*Ardea cinerea*), the diving, black CORMORANT (*Phalacrocorax carbo*), REDSHANK (*Tringa totanus*) and the red-beaked OYSTERCATCHER (*Haematopus ostralegus*).

You can also see the remains of old tidal mills about the estuarine creeks. Kinturley tidal cornmill was built at the beginning of the nineteenth century and tapped the energy of the fast tidal flows to grind the corn. Unfortunately this environmentally friendly form of technology has never been fully exploited even though such developments were first pioneered almost two centuries ago.

(6) Further along the green road the limestone begins to dominate and the unusual flowers of this alkaline habitat become more apparent. Patches of SPRING GENTIAN (*Gentiana verna*) and MOUNTAIN AVEN (*Dryas octopetala*) poke from the shattered rocks, surviving on the thin layer of soil trapped in the many crevices. Both the spring gentian and

the mountain avens are more often associated with the high Alps and the colder Arctic regions than with the mild and damp environment of the Burren, and thus their presence here has greatly puzzled botanists.

(7) As you follow the well-preserved green road for another 0.5ml/0.8km, watch for the rough outline of Tobar Phádraig (St Patrick's well) on the right.

The well is set back into the hill about fifty metres from the roadside and surrounded by rocky outcrops of limestone. Having percolated through the porous limestone of the hill, the water pours, pure and refreshing, from a metal spout. Interestingly, water that comes from a limestone area is generally referred to as hard water due to the high concentration of calcium hydrogen carbonate that becomes dissolved in it. Far from polluting the water, this gives it a better taste and is an ideal source of the calcium needed for healthy teeth and bones, especially for vegans who do not consume dairy products. The only drawbacks are the difficulty of forming a lather for washing and its tendency to deposit limestone and so block waterpipes. Near the well is a curious stone pillar, reputed to be an eighteenth-century memorial to the Comyn family.

The bee orchid is one of the many strange and delicate flowers found in the Burren.

(8) A few hundred metres beyond the well the green road begins to swing around to the right. Near here, keep a close watch for a break in the wall on the RIGHT, pass through the break and make your way across a small meadow towards the rocky escarpment that leads to the top of Abbey Hill.

In summer this meadow is coated with the purple flowerheads of COMMON KNAPWEED (*Centaurea nigra*), their tufted blossoms a favourite with bumblebees. There are well over a dozen species of bee found in Ireland but the ones most likely to be seen visiting the knapweed are the RED-TAILED BUMBLEBEE (*Bombus lapidarius*) and the strange CUCKOO BUMBLEBEE (*Psithyrus*), the latter so called because its habits are similar to those of the cuckoo bird. The female cuckoo bumblebee lays her eggs in the nest of other bees, leaving them to rear her larvae. As a result, cuckoo bees do not have the pollen baskets that would normally be used to store collected food for the growing brood. However, they have not lost the ability to sting!

(9) The cracked limestone terrain needs to be traversed with care as its many fissures can easily trip one up. But dangerous as they may be to the unwary, they provide the basis for the incredible collection of flowers found about the Burren.

Sheltered in cavities, several of the lime-loving orchids flower throughout the summer months. In April the first to appear is usually the EARLY-PURPLE ORCHID (*Orchis mascula*). Come May a cluster of the rarer species comes into bloom, such as the GREATER BUTTERFLY-ORCHID (*Platanthera chlorantha*), the FLY ORCHID (*Ophrys insectifera*), the PYRAMIDAL ORCHID (*Anacamptis pyramidalis*) and the extremely rare DENSE-FLOWERED ORCHID (*Neotinea maculata*). Throughout June and July you are likely to see the COMMON TWAYBLADE (*Listera ovata*) and the rare DARK-RED HELLEBORINE (*Epipactis atrorubens*). Finally, with the advent of August, the delicate white-flowered AUTUMN LADY'S TRESSES (*Spiranthes spiralis*) is in bloom.

Please do not be tempted to pick these as they are all protected. Even if you take the whole plant with the intention of planting it somewhere else, the exercise will be a failure. Orchids do not grow just anywhere and are dependent on the presence of a fungus within the soil to help them survive.

(10) At the first rise, the peaked cairn marking the summit of the hill becomes visible. Make your way as best you can towards this, climbing through and over the rock-scattered landscape.

As you climb you will encounter the occasional hollow within which a number of trees survive. Trees can etch out an existence on the Burren's limestone once the depredations of species like omnivorous goats and tree-felling humans are held at bay. However, despite the lack of trees here today, it is remarkable to find woodland plants thriving upon the naked limestone. In the cracks, fleshy leaved HART'S TONGUE FERN (*Phyllitis scolopendrium*), WOOD ANEMONE (*Anemone nemorosa*) and IVY (*Hedera helix*) grow beneath miniature trees and shrubs of WHITEBEAM (*Sorbus hibernica*), BLACKTHORN (*Prunus spinosa*) and HAZEL (*Corylus avellana*). The presence of these descendants of woodland species can only mean that more substantial woods did grow here once. We do know that PINE trees (*Pinus*) once dominated the heather-clad hills and it is quite probable that the more barren limestone was colonised by sporadic thickets of stunted HAZEL, YEW (*Taxus baccata*), BLACKTHORN and WHITEBEAM. But we can only guess at the overall extent of these woods and the true nature of the landscape before the arrival of humans will remain another one of the mysteries of the Burren.

(11) At the summit, the conical stone cairn protrudes from a stone wall on your left. Keeping the wall on your left, maintain a STRAIGHT course down the other side of the hill and follow the outline of the wall as it gradually swings to the right. Take care at the steep drops encountered on the way down.

The top of Abbey Hill is the ideal place for a break and a look at some of the many features of the Burren, especially its human antiquities. If you cross the stone wall and walk forward you should be able to spot the ruins of Corcomroe Cistercian Abbey nestled at the base of the hill and down to the right of the wooded farmland. Believed to have been founded in 1182 by Donal Mór O'Brien, it was given the illustrious name of St Maria de Petra Fertilis (St Mary of the fertile rock), a name which seems out of place in such a barren land – or perhaps this is a clue to the former landscape of the Burren. The ruins are certainly worth exploring as they contain some impressive architectural features and stone carvings. It also holds the royal tomb of Connor O'Brien with a carved effigy of the king lying on top of his last resting place.

Many other archaeological remains lie scattered about this broad valley. To the left of Corcomroe Abbey and beneath the distant Turlough Hill in the townland of Oughtmanna are the remains of an extensive collection of Early Christian churches. Finally, on top of Turlough Hill itself is an impressive collection of ancient hut sites and the remains of a hillfort, all of which date back to possibly the Iron Age about two and a half thousand years ago.

Such a large collection of important sites indicates that the area was once a thriving place of human habitation. However, one has to wonder at such a feverish concentration of people in such a barren land. Does it suggest that the area has indeed changed drastically from a more fertile state to its present impoverished one?

(12) Nearer the bottom of the hill watch for a break in the wall on your LEFT, just beside a small group of scrub and trees. Pass through the break in the wall and work your way down the steep incline with care as it is covered in high vegetation. One low stone wall will have to be crossed before emerging out onto the track.

(6) On reaching the track, you are back on the green road again. Go to the LEFT and follow the outward route back to the start of the walk (1).

Galway/Connemara

4 - Inishmore (Aran Islands)
Inis Mór (Árainn)

OUT OF THE WESTERN ATLANTIC OCEAN the islands of Aran erupt in sliding and splintered sheaths of stone to present all that is hauntingly real about the forlorn wilderness of Ireland's west coast. Stretched across the gaping mouth of Galway Bay the islands of Inis Mór (Árainn), Inis Meáin and Inis Oírr are bleak, windswept and constantly battered by the might of the Atlantic swell. Wizened by time and sculpted by the hands of innumerable generations, they are full of coloured pattern and light and possess a charm that is unsullied and unique.

Around Inis Mór, the untamed seas perpetually heave and roll like a boiling cauldron against its precipitous south-western perimeter, where the high wind-scoured hills and barren plateaus plunge over fearsome cliffs. A thunderous booming continually echoes from the watery depths to the stone-walled terraced fields above where the naked stones lie indifferent to the whine and pulsating surge of the ravenous sea below.

Despite the bleakness of its terrain, humans have inhabited Inis Mór back into the mists of time. During the pre-Christian era, its wild disposition would have served the needs of a warring people well, when defence was an important priority. Atop the forbidding cliffs lie the remains of ancient promontory forts that exploited both the isolation and the physical extremes of the island's topography. In later times a more relaxed people began to farm the barren rock, building up the soil over the centuries from a mix of sand and seaweed, then surrounding their small holdings with sheltering stone walls made from rock cleared from the meadows.

The isolation allowed the islanders to retain all that was rich and wholesome about themselves and their culture, absorbing the various waves of conquest that washed ashore. No doubt the islanders will also survive the present onslaught of tourism. But for now it gives a much-needed economic lift to a way of life that is as much under threat from world recession as any other quarter.

If you ignore the summer's sporadic and at times tidal wave of tourism, you can still find that spirit of island paradise which hints of pure wilderness, with its shrouding mists, cloud-filled skies and wave-lashed shores. Walking about the by-ways of Inis Mór, experiencing its barren rocks, shorn cliffs and rough seas so enchants that it cries out and claws at your soul. This isolated and untamed island quickly conquers and captivates your spirit.

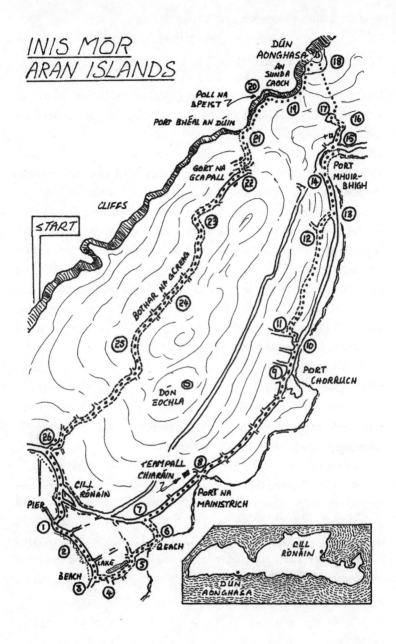

INIS MÓR
ARAN ISLANDS

DÚN AONGHASA

AN SUNDA CAOCH

POLL NA BPEIST

PORT BHÉAL AN DÚIN

GORT NA GCAPALL

CLIFFS

START

BÓTHAR NA GCREAG

DÚN EOCHLA

PORT MHUIR-BHIGH

PORT CHORRUCH

TEAMPALL CHIARÁIN

PORT NA MAINISTRICH

CILL RÓNÁIN

PIER

BEACH

LAKE

BEACH

CILL RÓNÁIN

DÚN AONGHASA

WALK DESCRIPTION

LOCATION: The walk starts by the pier of Cill Rónáin village on Inis Mór. Even though the island is accessible by ferry from Galway city, Doolin or Rossaveal, the times of the Rossaveal ferry suit this walk best.

TERRAIN: A moderate circular walk that follows the island's delightful green roads and crosses the top of its high cliffs. It is quite suitable for walkers who are reasonably fit. However, those with a fear of heights or accompanied by children should be aware of the exposed and dangerous nature of the cliffs. (See the note on cliffs in the Introduction.)

FEATURES: Limestone karst landscape; stone-walled meadows and green roads; wild flowers, rare plants and coastal wildlife; Early Christian ruins; Dún Aonghasa promontory fort; stunning cliffs and sea views; picturesque beach with views to Connemara.

LENGTH: 11.2ml/18km.

TIME: 5 hours. For those on a one-day visit to the island it is necessary to take the first Rossaveal ferry so as to finish the walk in time to catch the last ferry home – which is 6.30pm from June to September, allowing plenty of time, but is at 5pm from October to May, thus there is less time to waste and you must keep an eye on the time.

From Rossaveal the first ferry leaves at 10.30am. Allow 50 minutes for the crossing and be ready to start the walk at 11.30. To help you keep an eye on the time, if your visit is between October and May, try to be at point (14) by 2pm and leaving the fort of Dún Aonghasa at point (18) no later than 3pm.

NOTE: Return tickets can be purchased at the ferry terminal at €25 return. You must also pay €5 to park your car and it will cost you €3 to access Dún Aonghasa (2011 prices). It is worth checking the ferry website for updates and group/family prices at www.aranislandferries.com.

The island is also accessible by plane from Connemara airport at Inverin, but one needs to pre-book, tel: (091) 593034 or www.aerarannislands.com.

EQUIPMENT: Comfortable walking boots with a good grip. A knapsack for some food and additional clothing in case of rain or cold.

WHEN TO WALK: Suitable at any time of the year but best when the weather is mild and sunny. Avoid the cliffs during windy or misty weather.

NOTE: If you feel you are stuck for time during the walk, you can shorten it by going from point (10) to point (14) and also from point (15) to point (22). This latter short cut deletes Dún Aonghasa and follows the purple-arrowed walking pole markers for a loop walk called 'Lub chill Mhuirbhigh'.

The rasping call of the corncrake is a sound that is becoming increasingly rare in the countryside as its numbers decrease

WALK OUTLINE

(1) Having disembarked, walk up to the top of the long pier and take the road to the RIGHT. Pass down by the bicycle hire depots and follow the low-walled, tarred road along by the sea.

Arriving amidst crowds, jaunting cars, mini buses, the smells of rotting seaweed, horse dung and diesel, as well as facing a real danger of getting knocked down by a bike, you may wonder if this was really a good decision. But take your time, let the crowds disperse – most will head for the village of Cill Rónáin up to the left. Then you can move quietly off in the other direction.

(2) Very quickly you are beside the seashore. Continue STRAIGHT along the road until you come to the third left-hand turn.

If the tide is out the air reeks of decaying seaweed. This seaweed supports the insects which in turn draw the probing seabirds like the RINGED PLOVER (*Charadrius hiaticula*) and the TURNSTONE (*Arenaria interpres*). Far out to the right and across the distant waters, the stony hills of Burren country, their misty outline visible behind the nearby island lighthouse, signify the mainland of county Clare. Along the left-hand verge of the road the colourful blossoms of SEA CAMPION (*Silene maritima*), SWEET CHAMOMILE (*Chamaemelum nobile*) and SILVERWEED (*Potentilla anserina*) are in flower in mid-summer. Towards autumn watch out for the knobbly-looking seed heads of the SEA RADISH (*Raphanus maritimus*), the tall stands of SEA MAYWEED (*Matricaria maritima*) and MUGWORT (*Artemisia vulgaris*).

Inside the stone walls, the meadows are cluttered with the flowers of COMMON KNAPWEED (*Centaurea nigra*), HAWKWEEDS (*Hieracium*), ORCHIDS (*Dactylorhiza*), LADY'S BEDSTRAW (*Galium verum*), EYEBRIGHT (*Euphrasia*), CLOVER (*Trifolium repens*) and the delightful blue-belled flowers of the HAREBELL (*Campanula rotundifolia*).

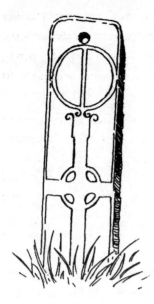

One of the strange cross-inscribed slabs that stand around the ruins of Timpeall Chiarán.

(3) Presently the coastal stretch gives way to a sandy beach, after which the third left-hand turn is reached. At this junction there is a walking sign in yellow pointing up to the LEFT. Take this LEFT turn and follow the stony track up through the maze of stone-walled fields.

Amidst the impressive web of loose stone walls, the wild flowers jostle for space as they push and shove before the light sea breeze. It is the total absence of intensive cultivation on the islands that has allowed these old meadows to retain their natural characteristics and support the increasingly rare CORNCRAKE (*Crex crex*), a bird now close to extinction throughout much of the mainland.

(4) After reaching a small lake on the left, you soon encounter a junction. Keep LEFT and follow the lake margin to its end to another Y-junction. Ignore one right-hand turn about mid-way along the lake.

You may spot an unusual square concrete structure in the fields. This is a water trough designed to suit the island's unique environment. Since the island is predominantly composed of porous limestone, wells and streams are rare and the all-too-frequent rain soaks away quickly, so the troughs were devised to catch as much rainwater as possible.

(5) On reaching the Y-junction at the top of the lake, turn RIGHT, following the track up between the high stone walls. Ignore the yellow arrow pointing to the left.

About here the meadows are dominated by the white-spoked flower heads of the tall GREATER BURNET SAXIFRAGE (*Pimpinella major*), which, like many of the calcicole or lime-loving plants, grows on the island in great abundance. And on calm sunny days the lane flutters with a variety of butterflies, such as the RED ADMIRAL (*Vanessa atalanta*), PEACOCK (*Inachis io*) and TORTOISESHELL (*Aglais urticae*). On top of the stone walls, STONECHATS (*Saxicola torquata*) perch, while flocks of STARLING (*Sturnus vulgaris*) skim from one meadow to the next.

(6) The lane leads up and out on to a fine sandy beach with impressive views across to the Connemara mountains. Cross the back of the strand and exit on to another stone-walled track that goes up to the LEFT.

Lying on the sheltered side of the island, the beach is well protected from the force of Atlantic currents. This keeps it relatively free of the plastic debris that has become so common on modern-day beaches. However, some plastic does appear, coming from passing ships and boats that naively dump their waste overboard. Unsightly as it may be, it is preferable to see it stranded on land rather than adrift on ocean currents where it causes incalculable damage to marine life. Adult birds mistake small fragmented particles of plastic for fish eggs and feed it to their young chicks; discarded ring packaging from beer cans chokes growing birds if they get it around their necks; similar bindings from fish cartons choke fish and seals, while whales and turtles ingest plastic bags believing them to be jellyfish. In all cases the outcome is a cruel death.

(7) The track quickly arrives on to a tarred road at a T-junction. Turn RIGHT, following the directions of the coloured arrow marker pole, paying particular attention to the purple one, called 'Lub chill Mhuirbhigh'.

Look across the meadows on the right to see the waters of Galway Bay stretch away eastward, bordered by the Twelve

The hoary rock-rose is one of the rarer flowering plants found on the Aran Islands.

Bens and Maumturk mountains to the north and the stony brow of Black Head to the south. If the road is particularly quiet you may be lucky enough to spot the small brown STOAT (*Mustela erminea hibernica*), which has a distinctive black tip to its tail. These predatory carnivores are intelligent and aggressive, moving silently about the stone-walled corridors in search of prey. Fearless, they are quite capable of taking on the much larger rabbit.

(8) Soon the road passes close to the seashore at Port na Mainistreach. Keep going STRAIGHT, passing a number of left turns, until Port Chorruch is reached.

Above you on the left are the ruins of Teampall Chiaráin (St Ciarán's Church). Accessible by a narrow track, the small ruin is surrounded by cross-inscribed stones that reflect the long history of Christianity on the island. From the fifth century to medieval times the Aran islands were important centres of religious devotion and learning. Numerous monks established primitive oratories here and their fame spread throughout the world, attracting many disciples, such as the founders of renowned monasteries like Clonmacnoise and Iona. Today many holy sites lie scattered over the island.

(9) You soon arrive at a small brackish lagoon separated from the open water by a stony spit. This is the bay of Port Chorruch and its adjacent lake. Continue STRAIGHT on from the spit for about 0.75ml/1km, until you come to the third lane on the left-hand side. Ignore any small tracks that lead into the adjoining meadows.

As you pass the first left turn, an old stone ruin flanks the roadside. These are the remains of a nineteenth-century seaweed fertiliser factory which exploited the rich crop of seaweed that could be harvested on this sheltered side of the island. Much of the seaweed was used for the production of iodine and also as a form of fertiliser, so crucial to maintaining the fertility of these man-made fields. While you walk, keep an eye on the water as there is a very good chance of seeing seals. Floating offshore and with just their snouts projecting above the water, they are easy to overlook. There are two species of seal and they can be hard to distinguish. However, their different breeding times can help to identify them – usually the COMMON SEAL (*Phoca vitulana*) – is absent during the summer as it moves to more secluded islands to give birth to its pups. GREY SEALS (*Malichoerus grypus*), on the other hand, breed in the late autumn and winter.

Nearer the shoreline rocks the pink flowers of SEA PINK (*Armeria maritima*) and the fleshy three-fingered leaves of ROCK SAMPHIRE (*Crithmum maritimum*) are easily spotted.

(10) On reaching the third lane to the left, highlighted by a black marker pole with coloured arrows, just a few metres beyond the entrance, go up to the LEFT between the high stone walls. The lane swings right and then left as it climbs the hill. Just before the brow of the hill, watch for an obscure footpath turning in on the right.

NOTE: If you want to save time, stay on the tarred road until you come to the sandy beach at point (14).

(11) The footpath is easy to miss as it branches off to the RIGHT through a break in the wall. This, however, is indicated by a black marker pole and its purple arrow, on the left-hand side of the lane, so keep an eye out for it. If you can see houses ahead you have missed the turn.

The path crosses a stretch of limestone pavement that beautifully displays many of the unique plants of this strange landscape. Composed of pure limestone, the Aran islands are an extended limestone reef of the fascinating karst region found on the Burren in county Clare. Thus Inis Mór has an equally impressive collection of limestone flora growing amidst the sheltered cracks and crevices of fractured limestone slabs. This prompted one of the twentieth century's most noted botanists, the Irishman Robert Lloyd Praeger, to state: 'On Aran the limestone pavement flora attains its most remarkable development.'

In spring and summer these barren-looking rocks hold a luxurious and rich mix of rare Alpine and Mediterranean species that is breathtaking.

Poll na bPéist may look enticing at low tide and when the sea is calm, but do not be fooled by appearances as strong currents surge through to it from underground passages!

Watch for Mediterranean species like the yellow-blossomed HOARY ROCK-ROSE (*Helianthemum canum*), the bright red BLOODY CRANE'S-BILL (*Geranium sanguineum*) and the white VERNAL SANDWORT (*Minuartia verna*). You will also find Arctic-Alpine species, such as IRISH EYEBRIGHT (*Euphrasia salisburgensis*), the spectacular, bright-blue SPRING GENTIAN (*Gentiana verna*) and the delicate MAIDENHAIR FERN (*Adiantum capillus-veneris*). You may spot the island's rarest plant PURPLE MILK-VETCH (*Astragalus danicus*), an Arctic species not found on the mainland, and possibly a survivor from post-Ice Age times.

(12) The open footpath eventually reaches a metal gate and runs back between stone walls to become a more marked path. This leads on to two Y-junctions – go down to the RIGHT at both and on to a tarred road.

(13) On reaching the roadway, go to the LEFT and follow it up to a sandy beach.

(14) At the beach of Port Mhuirbhigh, turn to the RIGHT, cross the beach and exit on to the road at the other side.

Search the beach as you cross and, depending on the currents, you may happen upon some stranded jellyfish. Usually there is quite a substantial number of jellyfish in the waters of Galway Bay, brought up from warmer southern climes by the summer ocean currents. They regularly get washed ashore with the high tide and it is easy to recognise common species like the brown-marked COMPASS (*Chrysaora isosceles*) and the light-purple COMMON AURELIA (*Aurelia aurita*) jellyfish.

(15) On stepping on to the road at the other side of the beach, cross it and take the side road that goes up STRAIGHT in front of you.

When crossing the road, beware of the high density of biking visitors, most of whom are heading for the promontory fort of Dún Aonghasa, providing you with an escort to the top.

NOTE: Hopefully you have reached here by 2pm. If you are stuck for time you can now take the following short cut: On the opposite side of the road is a large, sculptured sign post for Dún Aonghasa and also for Poll na bPéist. Take note of the laneway on your LEFT and signposted for 'Poll na bPéist'. It will also have the purple-arrowed marker pole for the loop walk of 'Lub chill Mhuirbhigh'. Follow this laneway and the purple-arrowed marker poles to reach point (22).

(16) The road leads up past a graveyard on your left and then goes around a sharp left-hand bend to pass the imposing building of Kilmurvey House on your right. Kilmurvey House is the former residence of the nineteenth-century island landlord Patrick O'Flaherty, who ruled with a tough hand and took possession of much of the arable land. Thus he was generally disliked by the islanders whose prayer was: 'From the ferocious O'Flaherty, Lord deliver us.'

Ignore the right-hand turn at the bend and follow the remainder of the road down to the car park and the Interpretive Centre – through which you must pass to gain access to Dún Aonghasa.

(17) A charge of €3 must be paid (2011). On exiting the rear of the building, a well-worn footpath leads up to the fort. Follow the path up to the cliff-tops across the fractured limestone terrain. The way is rough and stony and crosses over a number of stone walls by means of stiles, therefore take your time and watch your footing amidst the creviced rocks.

This area is usually crowded during the summer months, with a train of people winding up to the impressive promontory fort of Dun Aonghasa. Along the way, rich flower meadows survive between the rocky slabs and these are full of colourful blossoms that hum with the drone of bees in mid-summer. The many creviced grykes of the limestone also support the usual assemblage of unique flora, being well sheltered from the wind in these deep cracks, some of which can be up to 10ft/3m deep.

(18) On reaching the fort of Dún Aonghasa, turn LEFT and cross the stony ground towards the cliffs. Pass over a stone wall and then, with sensible caution and staying back from the cliff edge, head for the second indented bay of Port Bhéal an Dúin, visible in the distance.

Sitting on top of the impressive 300ft/90m cliffs, the fort is well defended by three semi-circular walls. It also has an outer *chevaux de frise* of sharp standing stones that would have been a serious obstacle to anyone trying to attack. It was obviously used for defence in a time of great conflict so that the islanders and warriors could hold off an attack from warring bands. The fort may not appear impressive at close range, looking like nothing more then a simple collection of stone walls, however, it is probably the finest

Now becoming increasingly rare, the traditional thatched Irish cottage
can still be seen in some parts of Inis Mór.

structure of its type in western Europe and its location on top of these wild cliffs adds to its drama. There is no record of details of the fort's builders or of its age, but some theories lead to a belief that it dates from the Bronze Age, about four thousand years ago, and may have been built by that mythical race, the Firbolgs, whose legendary leader was Aonghas. The Firbolgs were an ancient race who occupied Ireland and had their origins in Greece. They were later defeated by the Tuatha Dé Danann and the Milesians, one of whom was Queen Maeve whose love-child Conmaicne gave Connemara its name. Conmaicne was sent by the Gaelic chiefs to control and suppress the Firbolg people. He settled by the sea and his tribe became known as the Tribe of Conmaicne by the Sea – Conmaicnemara, which has since been shortened to Connemara.

(19) Beyond the fort the cliffs descend to the first bay, An Sunda Caoch (the blind sound). Please exercise CAUTION and on no account get too near the edge of the cliffs, especially if it is windy.

The views along the cliffs and over the rest of the island are impressive. The incredible maze of stone walls is highly prominent, running criss-cross over the limestone fields before plummeting over the windswept precipice. After a shipwreck, the waters around Blind Sound used to ensnare a lot of salvageable goods. Then the nineteenth-century islanders would climb down the cliffs by rope in order to collect valuable commodities such as timber, a very scarce material on this treeless island.

(20) On rounding the Sound, you come to a stone-splattered cliff-top. Take care as you follow the cliff line and keep an eye out for the curious Poll na bPéist (the worm hole).

The many heaps of boulders that litter the ground have not been tossed up here by the ocean. They are the remains of the shattered clifftop, blown back by wild gales which prevented them from falling into the sea. Poll na bPéist is easily recognised as it is a very large and perfect rectangular hole in the flat terrace at the bottom of the cliffs, not unlike a man-made swimming pool. It is connected to the sea by an underground passage through which the currents surge at high tide to meet the water pouring in over the top. As the tide ebbs, its enclosed waters swirl and boil, giving the impression that some large serpent is trapped within!

(21) Continue along the cliff-tops until the next bay is reached. This is Port Bhéal an Dúin (bay at the fort's mouth) and you must cross to its furthest side where you turn LEFT near some stone walls. The terrain along the shoreline is quite rough and will prove difficult to traverse, but keep going until you are below the houses on the far left. Then, scrambling up to the LEFT, you should encounter a rough track without walls which eventually leads out through a stile in a stone wall on to a better laneway. Follow the lane up to the village of Gort na gCapall (plot of the horses).

The high cliffs have levelled out considerably and there are the remains of a small slipway near the rocky shore. If the water is rough and wild, please exercise caution by not going too near the shoreline. Remember you are looking out on to the wild Atlantic and freak waves are a common occurrence during squally weather. It is worth remembering that it was on top of the high cliffs of Glassan Rock, further down the coast, that fifteen men from the village of Cill Éinne were swept to their deaths by a freak wave when they were fishing from the cliff-top for wrasse.

(22) On reaching the village the lane becomes tarred and leads down to a T-junction, with a commemorative garden dedicated to Liam O'Flaherty (2005). Go to the RIGHT and follow the road towards the distant maze of stone-walled fields.

NOTE: If you have come by way of the short cut from point (15), you arrive at the back of the cluster of houses, so work your way down to the junction with the commemorative garden and there go to the RIGHT.

This is the birthplace of the well-known novelist Liam O'Flaherty. He wrote in both English and Irish and encapsulated much of the now vanished island way of life in his writings. Many of the houses are now roofless, their original covering of thatch long gone. And gone too is an older way of life that though rich in culture was tough to endure, being completely isolated from the mainland. The romantic conditions of those earlier times, rather than the real, are well-portrayed in the classic film *Man of Aran*.

(23) Further on, the road reverts to a stony track that winds and weaves its way up through a delightful network of stone-walled fields.

Of all the monuments on these islands, from Bronze Age forts to Early Christian and pagan ruins, the most impressive must surely be the legacy of stone walls that were built by several generations over the previous centuries. A monument with no explanatory plaque that may confound the inhabitants of the future as much as the stones of Dún Aonghasa confound us today. The stone walls of the three islands run into several thousand miles and it is said that if they were lined up end-to-end the wall would run all the way across the ocean to America!

(24) Following the old track, you will meet three crossroads. Pass STRAIGHT through all of these and you eventually come to the top of a hill with views down into the bay of Cill Éinne.

The track is called Bóthar na gCreag, which means 'the road of the crags' and possibly refers to the rocky nature of the terrain through which it passes. As you wander through this empty wilderness of delightful meadows and grey limestone walls, with white puffy clouds rolling across the blue sky, you experience a sense of Aran that leaves an indelible mark upon your consciousness – a sense of place that is unforgettable and unique.

Along the track, SEA BINDWEED (*Calystegia soldanella*) and BURNET ROSE (*Rosa pimpinellifolia*) creep across the coarse limestone, small crops of BLACKBERRY (*Rubus*) lean against the walls and the twining strands of HONEYSUCKLE (*Lonicera periclymenum*) curl around the loose stones. The meadows overflow with their many blossoms, amongst which the SKYLARKS (*Alauda arvensis*) feed and hide. These birds fly up high to sing their characteristic tune on the finer days.

(25) At the brow of the hill, the village of Cill Rónáin and the starting point of the walk come into view across the bay.

Continue STRAIGHT down the hill, ignoring any turns until you come to a T-junction by the beached shoreline.

Over on your right is another promontory fort, Dún Dúchathair, while over on your left is the hilltop ring fort of Dún Eochla. Dún Dúchathair (the black fort) was originally the largest of the forts on the island and in its time must have been practically impregnable. Dún Eochla (the fort of Eochla) is another of the island's great ringforts and is littered all around with ancient remains.

(26) The track eventually becomes tarred and reaches a T-junction by the beach of Cockle Strand. Go to the LEFT along the main road and work your way back through the village of Cill Rónáin and down to the pier to catch the return ferry (1).

5 - Mount Gable

CONNEMARA IS A LAND OF BOG- DRAPED countryside that hangs in mighty folds from its central mountain mass. All around, expansive tracts of water-logged heath run in rippled folds to the foot of precipitous peaks that cast their towering shadows across the forlorn wasteland. The bleakness of the terrain has kept human population to a minimum and allowed the miles of abandoned countryside to retain a character where nature remains unbound.

Formed from the sedimented remains of plant material, bogs have little mineral wealth and are thus useless for agricultural purposes. Their main advantage to humans is the fuel they provide. But their importance to global ecology is more significant as they hold vast reserves of carbon dioxide, the gas which causes global warming. Sadly, bogs worldwide are vanishing fast, their fuel reserves going up in smoke, and the longterm consequences for the world's ecology seems unavoidable. Fortunately, one can still experience the beauty of these unique habitats on Ireland's west coast, with none as stunning as the bogs of west Galway.

In Connemara, there are many large and dangerous bogs where no path guides the way across the terrain of hillock and watery mire, where when the mists descend the way becomes a tortuous trek or comes to an unexpected end. Occasionally though, old turf roads lead into the wild bogs and allow one to touch the vanishing heart of this secret wilderness.

WALK DESCRIPTION

LOCATION: Situated in the heart of Joyce's Country, Mount Gable stands alone on the narrow strip of land that separates Lough Corrib from Lough Mask. On OS map No. 38 it is unnamed, other than its highest point at 416m which bears the name of Benlevy (Binn Shleibhe).

From the picturesque village of Clonbur (An Fhairche) travel a few hundred metres south on the R345 for Cornamona. If arriving in the village from Cong, go LEFT at the T-junction at the top of the village. Then take the first tarred road on the RIGHT. This minor side road has an adjacent stone plaque (embedded in the low stone wall surrounding the lawn of a new house) with an inscription in Irish welcoming you to Clonbur, 'Failte go dti an Fhairce'. Following this very narrow road keep RIGHT at the next three Y-junctions, then LEFT at a T-junction. Follow the road up-hill for a short distance, until a lay-by with a gate and stepped stile is met on the RIGHT. There is limited parking here. Do not obstruct private residences.

TERRAIN: This is an area of extensive sheep farming, thus NO DOGS.

Wet mountain heath accessible by means of an old bog road that leads to the expansive top of peat hags and watery hollows. A

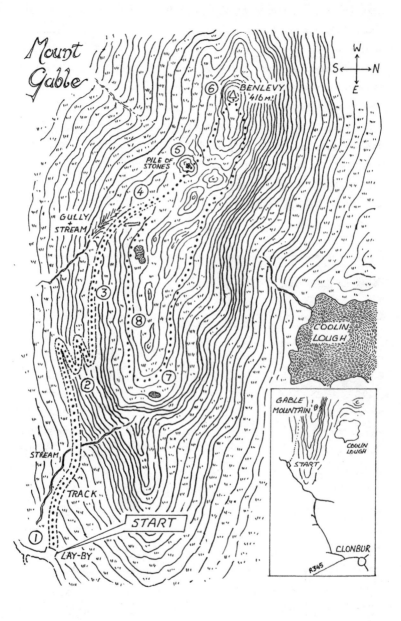

moderate, circular route is possible around the top of the mountain, however access and exit to the mountain-top are by the same route. Not to be attempted during low cloud or rain when the top is shrouded in mist.

FEATURES: Upland flora and fauna; spectacular views over Lough Corrib and Lough Mask and the adjacent mountainous Joyce Country.

LENGTH: 4 mls/6.5km, if one includes a circular route around the top. Additionally one could begin the walk in Clonbur, than the total length of the walk, out and back, would be 8 miles.

TIME: 3.5 hours if one walks at a casual speed and takes time to relax. If starting at Clonbur add on another 2.5 hours.

EQUIPMENT: Walking boots with ankle support and good grip. After rain, wellingtons are more suitable for the wet heath; Walking pole; The exposed top does not provide shelter thus suitable clothing is essential.

The delightful fluffy white heads of cottongrass billow across the wet heath in early summer.

WALK OUTLINE

(1) From the small lay-by climb the stepped stile and follow the grass-choked track as it climbs up through the rough heath (be careful of the stile as some steps are broken). On the left hand side a mountain stream gushes down in musical overtones from the ridge of Mount Gable that rises in front of you. As you rise the track becomes easily lost in the enclosing heath, however it climbs steadily going at an angle towards the LEFT-HAND-SIDE of the ridge.

All around a sea of rushy pasture blankets the lower slope. This may appear desolate and impoverished at first sight, but it has allowed a rich catalogue of heathland species to survive undisturbed. Luxuriant growths of COTTONGRASS, HEATHERS, SEDGES, and other moorland species pour from the wild rockeries to the laneway's edge. Watch for the white-tufted seed heads of COMMON COTTONGRASS (Eriophorum angustifolium) that appear in May and June. If you are lucky you may spot the rarer SLENDER COTTONGRASS (Eriophorum gracile), recognised by its three-angled stem. It is unique to the bogs of the west of Ireland.

(2) As the track rises it eventually zig zags twice before regaining its diagonal route to the top.

Behind, there are expansive views out over the island studded Lough Corrib that stretches south towards Galway City. Rising further, views to the left expose the upper reaches of the Lough as it winds in between the peninsular arm of Dooras and the delightful wooded groves of Doon Hill beyond. In the background the rising folds of the Mamturk Mountains both delight and amaze at their sudden appearance.

Keep an eye out for the delicate, lace-winged common blue damselfly near the water's edge.

(3) Nearing the top the track almost disappears in swards of rush. But following the narrow sheep track and the footprints of other walkers the better outline of the old road returns, it shortly passing beside a miniature gully on the left, down through which a stream pours.

About the short tufted wet heath you are bound to spot the small spoon-shaped leaves of the ROUND-LEAFED SUNDEW (Drosera rotundifolia) and its rarer cousin GREAT SUNDEW (Drosera anglica), with its elongated leaves. The leaves are covered with red hairs that secrete a sticky fluid on which insects become stuck and are then digested by the plants. The sundews are one of the three insect-eating groups of plants found in the bogs of Ireland.

(4) On reaching the top there is no sudden peak, but the track wanders in and across the flat top of Mount Gable. Looking diagonally to the LEFT a small pile of stones should be discernible atop a low mound on the distant visible horizon. Make for this, initially using the remains of the old track and later following the drier ground until the mound is reached. (If you cannot see it due to inclement weather than you should not be up here). On your right are the remnants of an old stone wall. Note this feature for the return journey when you need to descend from this same point.

The top of Mount Gable is characterised by an expanse of old turf cuttings, rising mounds and water filled hollows. Since it is not a very high peak when compared to the surrounding mountains, some vegetation can be found growing in the more permanent pools and streams, many of which are typical of the Connemara landscape. You may be able to recognise the thick swards of the beautiful ROYAL FERN (Osmunda regalis) that grow in large tufts on the banks, while on the water impressive sheets of WHITE and YELLOW WATER LILY (Nymphaea alba, nuphar lutea) float. You may also spot the strange-looking PIPEWORT (Eriocaulon aquaticum), which produces an unusual button-shaped white flower atop its leafless stem. It is not found on the European mainland but is a resident of temperate North America. Beside it you may see another curious resident, the WATER

LOBELIA *(Lobelia dortmanna)*, which would be more at home in the Alps. It may be identified by its cluster of bell-shaped pale lilac flowers. Both plants grow out of the water and come into flower from July to September.

(5) On reaching the mound with its pile of stones the true zenith of Mount Gable (or Benlevy) is visible across the watery heath to the north-west. This is marked by a concrete pillar and stands at a height of 416m. Make for this across the undulation terrain.

All around are the remains of former turf-cutting activity, which in many places has left the ground exposed and denuded. Very much a part of our Irish culture, this practice of using turf as fuel is ancient, providing a valuable source of energy when little else was available. However, after centuries of use, the bogs are now becoming rare and it is increasingly hard to find any in their pure state. Thankfully, a few of the more scientifically important, such as Roundstone bog, visible in the distance to the southwest, have now been given a limited degree of protection.

The brown, black-banded caterpillar of the oak eggar moth may be found amongst the leaves of the ling heather.

On the western seaboard of Ireland, most of the bogs are of the Atlantic blanket bog type as opposed to the raised bogs of the midlands. Some of these are quite old, dating back as far as ten thousand years. However, the larger tracts of blanket bog that exist in Connemara today began their formation about four thousand years ago. The weather must then have disimproved drastically, probably becoming even wetter and damper than it is now. This, in conjunction with the removal of aboriginal forests by the Neolithic peoples colonising Ireland, leached the soil, with an impermeable barrier forming lower down that kept the soil water-logged. These changes more than likely provoked the rapid spread of quick-growing, amphibious grasses and sedges, with each year's growth multiplying faster than it could decay, and so accumulating into thick blankets of spongy peat. By retaining the ever-falling rain and excluding all oxygen, the buried layers became preserved and compacted, while the upper living skin rose higher and higher. Thus after several thousand years it formed peaty deposits of up to perhaps 20ft/6m deep, and in some cases 40ft/12m, like some of the raised bogs in neighbouring county Offaly.

The bladderwort's yellow blooms project above the water, while its more sinister tendril-like leaves and battery of small insect-eating bladders lie submerged underneath.

(6) On reaching the concrete pillar at the true zenith, continue clockwise around the top to eventually arrive at the eastern edge of Mount Gable. From there continue the clockwise motion until you arrive back at the old bog road by which you ascended.

From the zenith point the surrounding mountains are impressive in their mass. To the north are the flat topped Partry Mountains, the location of walk No. 12, Lough Nadirkmore. To the west the lower hills of Joyces County run to the impressive massiffs of the Maumturks and the Twelve Bens behind them. Looking southwest the expansive water filled bogs of Rounstone are visible as they stretch away to distant hills and the sea.

(7) Arriving at the eastern edge fabulous vistas across the expansive plains of Mayo unfold.

Directly below the northern edge of Mount Gable sits the picturesque Coolin Lough. Further afield, Lough Mask stretches away to the north east, while Lough Corrib lies to the southeast. No visible river connects these two extensive freshwater lakes. As the area is composed of limestone the water drains from one to another through a number of subterranean passages. The change in terrain over this eastern prospect is dramatically different from the views to the west. Extensive farmland interspersed with several lakes runs north eastwards towards the town of Ballinrobe, renowned fishing country.

(8) As you travel back towards point (4) you should once again have clear views back down over the wooded shores of Lough Corrib, now on your left.

As you walk, you are bound to flush out some of the small heathland moths that dive quickly back into the vegetation. Most insects in this exposed habitat prefer to stay well hidden so that at first you may think that the habitat is not in any way productive. However, though the number of species is reduced, there is a rich invertebrate fauna of SPIDERS, TICKS, GRASSHOPPERS, and BEETLES that hide within the low vegetation. In summer, look out for the various species of caterpillar, some quite large like the OAK EGGAR *(Lasiocampa quercus)* whose brown larvae feed on LING HEATHER.

Do not be surprised by the sudden darting of the SNIPE *(Gallinago gallinago)* from the heath as you approach. A familiar bird of the bog, the snipe makes a most unusual drumming sound with its tail feathers as it flies high over the bog during the breeding season.

(4) Having arrived back at the old bog road return by the outward route, but be wary of the slippery and steep descent especially after wet weather.

As you descend watch the track-side drains and pools for the rubbery-leaved white-flowered BOGBEAN *(Menyanthes trifoliata)* and the less conspicuous BLADDERWORT *(Utricularia)*, another insect-eater.

6 - Errisbeg Mountain

THE BROAD EXPANSE OF SEA around Connemara has played a significant role in the development of human settlements down through the centuries. A land dominated by an extensive mantle of bog draped around a series of precipitous quartzite peaks made mobility in former times – by horse and foot – extremely difficult. Thus the sea became the highway of Connemara and the communities that evolved clung to the more sheltered corners of its indented coastline.

During medieval times, the inhospitable west of Ireland maintained not only a physical isolation from the rest of the country but also an economic one. The resident ruling Celtic tribe, the O'Flahertys, and the twelfth-century Norman settlers who had become absorbed into Gaelic society, developed a lucrative trade between Connemara and the continent. By the fourteenth century, Connemara had become an almost autonomous kingdom completely free of colonial interference. The O'Flahertys and the neighbouring O'Malleys and Burkes had substantial fleets of ships that traded with Flanders, France, Portugal and Spain, while Galway city, the 'City of the Tribes' produced its own governing body and mint.

But such opulence and wealth could not escape the notice of the invading colonialists, who used brute savagery to smash the region's independence and bring it under their own control. But troubled times always generate their heroes and Connemara had none more dashing and brave than the high-spirited 'Queen of Connemara', Granuaile, or Grace O'Malley. Through marriage she allied the O'Malleys with the O'Flahertys and Burkes to form a united force against the invading powers. Sadly, this was to no avail as the military campaign and Reformation of Elizabeth I destroyed everything, laying waste the West's people, economy and culture. Broken-spirited, Granuaile eventually died on Clare Island, while the Celtic way of life lay tattered, and utterly changed for evermore.

Standing high above the Connemara landscape, you can look down and see where this epic saga unfolded. By the fishing village of Roundstone the high peak of Errisbeg Mountain gives fine views over the island-spattered, coastal seas. Here one can imagine the fleets of trading ships that plied in and out of Galway Bay en route from the continent, while many more would lie anchored in the sheltered bays by the homes of the ruling families. Behind Errisbeg the impressive views vividly show the stark bleakness of the bogs and the enclosing mountains that ensured the independence of this medieval principality for all of two hundred years.

ERRISBEG MOUNTAIN

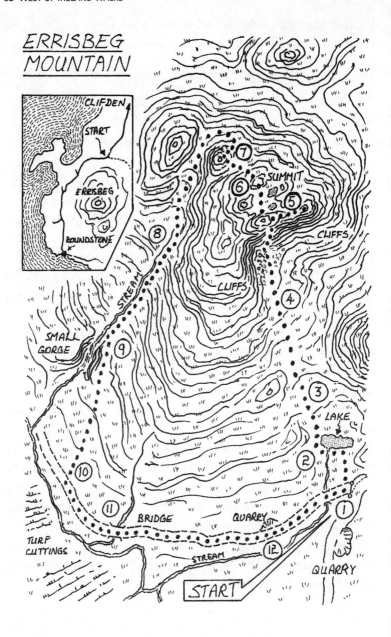

WALK DESCRIPTION

LOCATION: Travel west from Roundstone along the Roundstone-Clifden road for about 3ml/5km. On a sharp left-hand bend a track with a steel gate branches off to the RIGHT beneath the folds of Errisbeg mountain. Sensible but limited parking is available here. Be careful of the heavier tourist traffic when crossing the road during the busy summer season.

TERRAIN: A tough climb to the top of this low mountain (987ft/300m). The circular route crosses the rough and, at times, steep terraced heath with no clear path. A walk for the more experienced, thus a previous knowledge of mountain terrain is essential.

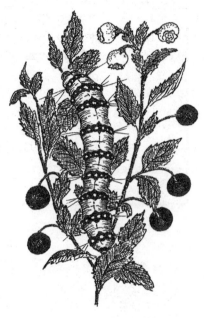

Watch out for the green, black-banded caterpillar of the emperor moth amongst the bilberry bushes.

FEATURES: Mountain heath; associated flora and fauna; splendid views of the indented coastline and Galway Bay to the south; stunning views over the unique Roundstone bog as well as the fortress Twelve Bens and Maumturk mountains to the north.

LENGTH: Approximately 3ml/5km, but make allowance for the rough terrain and contoured incline which make the walk feel almost twice as long.

TIME: 3 hours.

EQUIPMENT: Strong waterproof boots with a good grip. A knapsack for additional clothing and some refreshments. A compass is desirable.

WHEN TO WALK: Suitable at any time of the year but on no account should the walk be attempted when there is a risk of mist or rain and its associated low cloud descending on the mountain-top. Should not be attempted alone. **Warning: This is sheep-rearing country – on no account bring dogs onto the hills. Too many walks are being blocked by distressed landowners because of this.**

WALK OUTLINE

(1) Having parked and located the laneway, pass through the gate and go immediately to the RIGHT, off the lane. Walk up across the heath and work your way towards the high rocky ridge of Errisbeg ahead.

Clumps of stunted BELL HEATHER (*Erica cinerea*) and dwarfed AUTUMN GORSE (*Ulex gallii*) half-cloak the many boulders littered about the pockets of shorn grass. Both a blaze of colour in September, these hardy shrubs form the base of the restricted food chains of these generally impoverished hills. They provide cover for nesting birds and a large diversity of insects, many of which are unique to this harsh habitat. Watch for the fat grubs of certain moths that feed on the heather during the summer months. The beautiful yellow jewelled, black-banded green larvae of the EMPEROR MOTH (*Saturnia pavonia*) can be as big as your forefinger.

(2) Very shortly, you come to a small lake dammed with an artificial stone embankment. Go clockwise around to the LEFT, crossing the outlet stream and then turn up RIGHT by the left-hand side of the lake.

The lake was dammed in the last century as a source of water for the nearby but now disused mines. A closer look at the impounded waters will introduce you to some interesting residents. As well as native pondweeds, you may spot some thin green spikes projecting from the water with simple button-shaped flowers on top. Large carpets of these tend to occur on the right-hand side of the lake. This is PIPEWORT (*Eriocaulon aquaticum*), a native of North America, but alive and well in this Irish bog. On the left-hand side of the lake, the reddish stems of WATER LOBELIA (*Lobelia dortmanna*), another lost migrant more at home in the Alps, stick up out of the shallows. It is most probable that they are both survivors from post-glacial times when a montane-type climate affected Ireland.

(3) Maintain a STRAIGHT course towards the rocky mountain ahead. Stick to a central course between the flanking hills, at times following rough sheep paths.

As you start to ascend, fine views of the coast begin to develop. Looking west over your left shoulder, you can see Slyne Head at the end of the next promontory of Ballyconnelly. On the promontory sits the lone high hill of Bunowen; at its base lived Granuaile with her husband Donal O'Flaherty in the now-demolished Bunowen Castle, and they kept their fleet of ships anchored in nearby Bunowen Bay.

The isolation of this mini-state proved little defence against Elizabeth I's Lord Presidents of Connaught, first Sir Edward Fitton, and later Sir Richard Bingham. During the terrible years of the late sixteenth century, wholescale looting and destruction occurred. Churches were stripped of their riches and many of their ancient manuscripts were destroyed. Crops were burnt and cattle and horses seized. Priests were executed, most of the old Gaelic leaders were hanged in Galway city and thousands were exported to the East Indies where they became known as 'white negroes'. Those that remained suffered from famine as thousands more throughout Ireland were driven from their ancestral lands and forced to Connemara, the only place they were allowed to remain. Starved and semi-naked many of them died by the roadside, leaving orphaned children as prey for the wild wolves. Thus to this very day the fearsome words of 'to hell or to Connaught' are well known to every Irish person.

(4) Aim for the gradual slope in the centre of the ridge STRAIGHT ahead. As you climb, keep to the higher ground on the left, avoiding the lower ground to the right. You soon approach a cliffed ascent with a jumble of

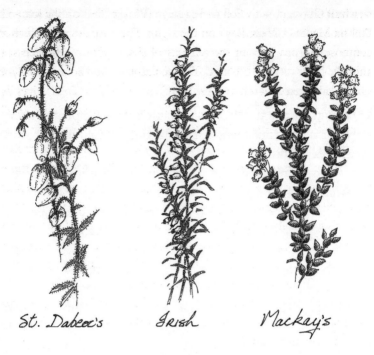

St. Dabeo's   Irish   Mackay's

These three types of heather are primarily confined to the wet bogs of Connemara and Mayo, making these habitats extremely rare, unique and important.

shattered rock and boulders cascading down on the left. You must use a certain amount of initiative to pick the easiest route to the top.

Lower callows are water-logged but within them may be found the insect-eating SUNDEW (*Drosera rotundifolia*). Overhead, GREY CROWS (*Corvus corone corone*) soar around the steep peak as they seek carrion. On windless days their raucous lonesome tones give an atmosphere of abandonment to the desolate landscape.

(5) On arriving on top of the first peak you will discover that there are several rocky hillocks crowning the top. The real summit, however, has a white concrete pillar. Make for this across the undulating stony ridge, avoiding the occasional small pool.

But first, walk out to the edge of the nearest peak on the right to take in the panoramic views of the coastline. Below you is the beautiful sandy beach of Gorteen, with Poll na Feadóige (Plover Bay) on the left and Poll na Madraí (Dogs' Bay) on the right. The particles of sand that compose the beaches are the remains of shells from small deep sea animals called FORAMINIFERA. The peninsular tombolo is actually a small island linked to the mainland by these sandy deposits. It gives its name to Errisbeg mountain, or in Irish 'Iorras Beag', which means 'small penninsula'. Across Bertraghboy Bay on your left and south to the tip of the next peninsula of Carna or Iorras Aintheach (the stormy peninsula), you may spot the small offshore island of St Mac Dara. One of the more famous islands of this region, it was the sixth-century hermitage of St Mac Dara, the patron saint of south Connemara's fishermen. The island still holds his spectacular church, likened by some to a miniature Inca building because of its massive interlocking stone walls and stone roof. For centuries, fishermen passing the island would dip their sails three times – believing that those who did not would incur the saint's anger.

Another bit of folklore relates to the small pools found on this mountain-top: it is said that should you bathe in them, your hair will immediately turn white!

(6) On reaching the top, marked by the concrete pillar, turn your back to the sea and look across the right-hand side of Roundstone bog, towards the edge of the Twelve Bens mountains and north-eastwards towards the Maumturk mountains. Here you will see another stony peak a few hundred metres away blocking a clear view of the Maumturks. Make for this, and you should find it crowned with a small stone cairn.

But first witness the spectacular view from the concrete pillar by looking northward across the expansive Roundstone bog and up to the Twelve Bens mountains. Roundstone bog, with its complex maze of lakes, is not only fabulous to behold from this vantage point but is also a site of particular interest to botanists, as a number of unusual plants are found there. It is one of the few locations outside the Pyrenees where MACKAY'S HEATH *(Erica mackaiana)* is found. The rarer ST DABEOC'S HEATH *(Daboecia cantabrica)* and IRISH HEATH *(Erica erigena)* also occur, mixed in with the common and widely distributed CROSS-LEAVED HEATH (*Erica tetralix*) and LING (*Calluna vulgaris*). This is an extraordinary group of heathers which belongs to the mysterious Hiberno-Lusitanian group of plants that are of Pyrenean-Mediterranean origin, and may be survivors from post-glacial times. To see them hanging in such profusion over the lake margins, from which protrude the American PIPEWORT (*Eriocaulon aquaticum*) and the Alpine WATER LOBELIA (*Lobelia dortmanna*) is a classic picture for any botanist.

Looking across the bog to your left and in the direction of Clifden, you see the bogland of Derrigimlagh, the site of Marconi's first transatlantic wireless station. Nearby is the landing site of Alcock and Browne, the first men to fly across the Atlantic on 15 June 1919.

The wheatear has a distinctive black and white tail pattern that is easily spotted both in flight and when perching.

(7) Having reached the peak marked with the stone cairn, climb down the drop on its eastern side, going in a curve to the RIGHT. When you get into the bottom of the small valley, swing LEFT, heading down towards Roundstone bog. Keep a central course between the two opposing ridges.

Before you leave, pause to capture the uninterrupted and spectacular views north-eastwards to the mighty mountain masses. Bleached white, the steep quartzite peaks of the Twelve Bens run from Clifden in the north west across the back of the bog to meet the ridged peaks of the Maumturks. Of pre-Cambrian origin they are some of the first rocks to give rise to present-day Ireland, possibly six hundred million years old. During good weather when their jagged peaks poke the blue cloud-scattered sky, they form an incredibly beautiful vista that is hard to match anywhere on these islands.

(8) Keep descending through the heath until a stream is met. It is best to follow its course downwards until you arrive near the base of the mountain.

The flatter stretches are boggy and wet but because this area is more sheltered from the sea there is a richer growth of ferns and heather on the slopes. Keep your eyes open here for MACKAY'S HEATH (*Erica mackaiana*), which is rather low in size and has pale pink-purple flowers that open in August and September. You may also spot the similarly coloured IRISH HEATH (*Erica erigena*), but this is much taller and bushier and has male anthers protruding from its bell-shaped flowers which bloom during April and May. The easiest to recognise is ST DABEOC'S HEATH (*Daboecia cantabrica*), with its extraordinary large pink flowers that appear in summer.

(9) When the stream drops into a picturesque mini-gorge, start swinging to the LEFT, at the same time gradually climbing down to the mountain base. Down to the right by the lakes, you will see some abandoned turf cuttings, ignore these and make for another series of turf cuttings STRAIGHT ahead. You should ultimately come out on to the turf cutters' track.

On a fine summer's day, if you look across the broad expanse of bog to the right, the warm smell of turf and heath drift upwards on the pristine air while a sparkling blue sky reflects from the myriad of acid-brown pools that stretch away into the infinite wilderness. The sense of freedom in the land's openness is exhilarating and gives a tired and over-stressed soul a refreshing boost. To cross these bogs where neither road nor house exist would be quite an arduous task. But it is nice to think that there is a place where society cannot intrude and nature is left to her own devices, free from the imposition of humans.

Sadly, this may not always to be the case. Roundstone bog is now the subject of heated debate between the usual opponents – conservationist and developer. To some, the bog is an unusable bit of flat ground of no benefit to society, and so the ideal site for an airport. In this way, it is hoped to increase the number of tourists into the area and so reduce unemployment. A noble aim but perhaps a misguided one. Why do so many tourists want to come here in the first place? For me the answer is quite simple: it is a wild, abandoned, beautiful, unspoiled landscape where one can escape from the intense, noisy, polluted, over-commercialised world. To put an airport here would destroy the area's very soul, removing another of the last few refuges of nature and, in the process, mortally wounding the area's tourism potential. In one sense the problem is carried over from the past when Connemara's isolation was felt just as deeply. But in the days of Granuaile, this isolation was turned to Connemara's advantage, making it and Galway city quite a wealthy principality. Surely, like its past, Connemara's future lies in its isolation and every effort should be made to retain it.

(10) On reaching the track go to the LEFT.

The lane meanders between rocky outcrops and grassy heath. Keep a lookout for STONECHATS (*Saxicola torquata*) and WHEATEARS (*Oenanthe oenanthe*) during summer months. These small songbirds feed upon the many insects that abound amongst the heathland thickets. When disturbed by your arrival, they dart to the safety of the protruding rocky outposts to await your closely watched departure.

(11) Later the track crosses over a small bridge and winds its way around the mountain base.

In previous editions of this book I referred to an unsightly dump encountered along the track. Thankfully some thoughtful individual(s) have since removed this, demonstrating a more educated attitude towards our pristine environment. Well done. Hopefully many will copy their example as we all help to tackle the problem of waste created by us in our excessive consumer society.

(12) Nearing the end of the track, you pass a small open quarry, the site of now-unused copper mines. These were quarried in the mid-nineteenth century, the water for processing the ore being channelled down from the dammed lake met at point (2) on the outward route.

(1) Quite shortly, the track arrives back at the steel gate and the parked car.

7 - Maumturk Mountains

TO WANDER UNFETTERED AMIDST the wild and desolate mountaintops is definitely to experience the ultimate in walking. In the last bastion of land-based wilderness, an untamed world unfolds that is far removed from the realm of humankind. It is a land of high relief, full of towering peaks, expansive mountain plains, cliff-edged corries and trails of meandering ridges that run in a confused maze around the ensnared valleys. The mountains are a magical place that can be both cruel or kind, but are always full of romance.

Up in the lofty peaks, one gazes over a three-dimensional map of land and sea that stretches out far below, where vistas lie exposed that are more rolling cloud-filled sky than solid earth. On rainy days, one watches the thunderous volumes of darkened grey-white cloud rise in billowing towers from the metallic surface of an angry ocean, as if from some enormous volcano hidden over the edge of the earth. Out of the ruptured base of melting clouds, rainbowed showers and veiled mists fall, to rush across the prairie-like expanse of waterlogged bog and escape to the safety of the mountainous mass. On brighter days, the overpowering sun sends puncturing shafts of light through the cloud-roofed sky, scattering the shattered cloud remains to the heavens, while the shadows of their retreating forms race like galloping steeds across the mighty mountain slopes.

Climbing to the high uplands away from all but the minimum of human interference is a challenge that comes close to an expedition to some uncharted isle. But such regions do not offer their rewards lightly and one must travel prepared for the harshness of mountain terrain. Abandoned as this place is, several days may pass before another person comes your way. The high cliffs and mountain peaks dictate where you may wander. Unexpected bad weather can develop quickly, drowning the upper mountain levels in low cloud and engulfing you in a mist of blinding fog, leaving you to stray frantically through the monotonous heath for hours on end, or worse, over the edge of some steep ravine. The mountains, like the sea, are bewitching, but can be horribly cruel and violent.

WALK DESCRIPTION

LOCATION: The Maumturk mountains run for 20ml/32km from Maam Cross in the south to Leenane in the north. The walk crosses through their central mass and begins at the car park of the holy shrine of Máméan – St Patrick's bed and well.

From Maam Cross travel the Maam Cross-Clifden road for 6.5ml/10.4km towards Recess. Less than 1ml/1.6km before Recess watch for a RIGHT turn, where a small sign reads: 'Máméan. Tobar +

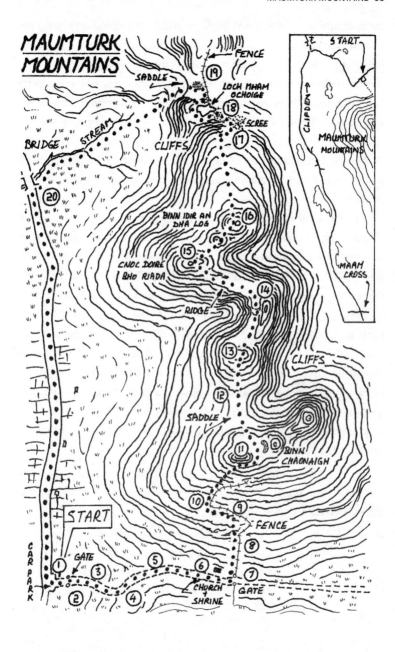

MAUMTURK
MOUNTAINS

SADDLE

FENCE

LOCH MHAM
OCHOIGE

SCREE

CLIFFS

BRIDGE

STREAM

CLIPDEN

START

MAUMTURK
MOUNTAINS

MAAM
CROSS

BINN IDIR AN
DHA LOG

CNOC DOIRE
BHO RIADA

RIDGE

CLIFFS

SADDLE

BINN
CHAONAIGH

START

FENCE

GATE

CAR PARK

GATE

CHURCH
SHRINE

leaba Phádraig'. If you cross a bridge and pass a church you have just missed the turn off. When coming from Clifden this turn off will be on the LEFT, approximately 23km/16m from Clifden.

Follow the side road STRAIGHT for the next 2ml/3.2km, ignoring any left turn-off. The road climbs gradually to the mountain base and after a sharp left-hand bend brings you to the rough car park on your RIGHT.

TERRAIN: Mountain-tops rising to 2307ft/703m. This is an extremely tough circular walk over a very strenuous route. The walk travels along the central ridge of the Maumturks and returns by way of a minor road. There are several peaks to be climbed, which are surrounded by dangerously steep sides and cliffed ravines. To negotiate such terrain requires a sound understanding and experience of such features and an ability to trust to your instincts on changing weather conditions. On no account enter the high mountains on your own.

FEATURES: The Maumturk mountains; geological and glacial features; Alpine flora; upland wildlife; St Patrick's bed and well; incredible views over vast stretches of Connemara, including its expansive boglands, indented coastline and the Atlantic ocean; fine vistas of the Twelve Bens mountains, the picturesque Inagh valley, Joyce Country and the mountains of south Mayo.

LENGTH: 9.5ml/15km. This does not take into account the undulating terrain which will make the walk seem longer.

TIME: A minimum of 7 hours at a comfortable pace. Normally, allow roughly one hour to the mile for tough walking, which constitutes 6mls/10km of this walk; the remainder is on the access roads.

EQUIPMENT: As this is not a walk for the amateur, it requires specialist mountain gear. Strong mountain boots and appropriate clothing for cold or wet conditions are essential. Remember that for every hundred-metre rise above sea level there is a one-degree drop in temperature, thus when it is seven degrees at sea level it is at freezing point on the mountain-top. Also carry a knapsack for spare clothes, food, first aid kit, compass, whistle and reliable ordnance survey maps.

Always let someone know where you have gone and what time you expect to be back.

WHEN TO WALK: Any time of the year, depending on the weather conditions. The long days of summer allow more time, but may bring wet and overcast weather which makes the peaks inaccessible. In autumn and early spring, despite having shorter days and less time to dawdle, you are guaranteed colder and drier weather with frosty skies and crystal clear views. Avoid snow when it does occur if you are not accustomed to this condition. Similarly, strong winds are trying.

WALK OUTLINE

(1) From the car park a stony path leads up to the mountains behind. Follow this UP to an iron-barred gate.

The old track leads up over the low pass of Mámean (pass of the birds), which crosses the backbone of the Maumturk mountains (Máim Tuirc – pass of the boars). It is an extremely old route, dating back to pre-Christian times when it was an access point to Connemara and possibly the site of pagan rituals.

(2) On reaching the gate pass through and reclose it after you.

The gate has the word 'Mámean' inscribed on it and bears a small cross on top. The track leads to the ancient pilgrimage site of the holy well and bed of St Patrick, which forms the focal point of an important religious pattern (the Stations of the Cross). An annual pilgrimage, which dates back to the fifth century, takes place here in August.

(3) A crude outline of stones flanks the old path as it climbs upwards.

Since the hills are exposed to the elements, the Maumturks are subject to high winds and low temperatures. This, in conjunction with the acidic nature of the bedrock, ensures that little of the usual lowland vegetation can thrive. Any that does occur is sparse, and confined to peaty clumps between sheets of white rock. Instead, a number of hardier Alpine plants tend to flourish in the harsh conditions, with some even occurring on the higher peaks. It is predominantly the grass-like SEDGES (*Carex*) and stunted HEATHERS (*Erica*) that are found on these lower slopes.

(4) Higher up, the path swings gradually to the LEFT and the bleached bones of the first summit to be climbed rises up before you on the left. This is known as Cnoc Doire Bhéal an Mháma (the mountain of the wood at the mouth of the pass).

Turn around and look back to see the expansive views already opening up. On your right the tall pyramidal stacks of the Twelve Bens mountains run down on to a great flat boggy plain. This sweeps across to your left and stretches away south to the sea near the peninsula of Kilkeran.

(5) The path begins to level out towards the top of the pass but becomes indistinct further on where one has to clamber over some of the protruding rocks. Maintain a STRAIGHT course and presently you should see a small church beneath the distant cliff on your left.

On windless days, there is a pleasant silence about this spot. The only sound is the echo of your footsteps from the cliff-edged amphitheatre and the hushed gurgling of distant streams spilling through the peat-smothered gullies.

St Patrick's cabbage growing from a bed of wood sorrel leaves. Both can be found in the sheltered rock crevices on the mountainside.

(6) On arriving at the holy shrine you must climb up the rocky slope on your left to visit

St Patrick's bed and holy well. However, the most comfortable way up to the mountain summit is to continue STRAIGHT on along the track for a few hundred metres until you reach a wire fence with an iron-barred gate.

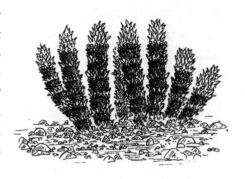

Fir clubmoss will be found growing in small green-tufted clumps on the rocky stone-spattered peaks.

The shrine consists of a small church, a rocky cleft which was used as an altar or Mass rock, St Patrick's bed, the holy well and a circular enclosure of stones which represent the Stations of the Cross. The Mass rock would have been used during Penal times in the eighteenth century when the practice of Catholism was banned.

Within the stone enclosure a series of rites is carried out in the form of a pattern (*pátrún* – patron saint); prayers are said and crosses inscribed on stones with a small rock as the pilgrim moves about the enclosure. For centuries the pilgrimage to Mámean has been held annually to commemorate the time St Patrick is said to have climbed Mámean to see and bless Connemara. When he reached the top and saw the forbidding Twelve Bens and the vast wild plain of the lowlands stretching away to the coastal archipelago, he is reputed to have said: 'Well, I'll bless you anyway but sorra foot I'll set upon you.' But it is more probable that his visit coincided with the intention of replacing an old pagan ritual with a new Christian one.

The pattern fell into disrepute during the early nineteenth century when it developed into a festive occasion of drinking, singing, laughing, fiddling, piping and the harmless sport of faction fighting. In this sport, disputing families fell upon each other in mock battle, with shillelaghs clashing amidst much shouting and screaming. It is said that few if any injuries were ever sustained!

(7) On reaching the iron-barred gate do not cross over it but go to the LEFT and follow the line of the fence as it climbs up through the rocky incline. The climb is over a jumbled collection of rocks and small cliffs but in general it is quite easy. Keep your hands free and stay near the fence.

Amongst the rocks, sheltered clefts allow the growth of a few unusual residents. Watch for the appropriately named ST PATRICK'S CABBAGE (*Saxifraga spathularis*), a rare plant that is mostly confined to the west of Ireland. You may also spot a few COMMON DOG VIOLET (*Viola riviniana*), and WOOD SORREL (*Oxalis acetosella*). It is unusual to find these latter plants up here as their preferred habitat is woodland. Their presence suggests that they may be left-overs from the woods which once occurred here and from which this mountain takes its name (see point 4).

(8) As you climb upwards, the rocky escarpments increase and you should notice when the fence begins to swing away to the right. At this point, leave the wire fence and keep going STRAIGHT, climbing up over a low cliff. Once on top of the shattered white rocks maintain a STRAIGHT course until you meet the wire fence again.

Looking to the right, you find increasingly better views down into the glaciated valley of Gleann Fhada (the long glen), then out to the Maum valley and across to the distant shores of Lough Corrib, that great body of water separating the fertile plains of east Galway from the rugged wilderness of its western seaboard.

The Alpine conditions are now becoming more marked, thus you may notice the gradual appearance of a short tufted plant growing amongst the rock-splattered terrain. This is FIR CLUBMOSS (*Lycopodium selago*), one of the few Alpine-type plants that occupy the high mountain-tops and not generally found in the lowlands. Alpine plants are quite rare and very poorly represented in Ireland, and they grow best on high north-facing aspects. Again, they are possible left-overs from post-glacial times when the climate was more Arctic-Alpine, allowing these plants to be much more widespread.

Other rare Alpine plants found on the Maumturks are ALPINE CLUBMOSS (*Lycopodium alpinum*), ALPINE MEADOW-RUE (*Thalictrum alpinum*) and JUNIPER (*Juniperus communis*), all of which grow in sheltered pockets in the scree-strewn landscape of the upper mountain-tops.

(9) Very soon you meet the wire fence again as it crosses your path from the right. Go to the LEFT with the fence until the Twelve Bens come back into view, then swing RIGHT and uphill with the fence, stopping when it again runs away to the right at point (10).

When you look back over the southern end of the Maumturk mountain chain, the Aran islands should be visible. Nearer home, many sea inlets that surround the archipelago of Rossaveal and Gorumna Island sparkle.

(10) As you climb upwards the fence comes to an end, swinging sharply off to the right. Keep going STRAIGHT to reach the summit. This is visible ahead, distinguished by a large white round-domed rocky knoll of bare quartzite. On reaching the knoll, you can gain the summit by going up to the left or the right of it.

(11) At the top, walk at an angle to the LEFT (north-west) across the stone-shattered plateau of Binn Chaonaigh which means 'mossy peak' – this may relate to the large amount of ALPINE CLUBMOSS (*Lycopodium alpinum*) that grows about the scree. Keep the small lake, at the back of which is the true summit, well over to your right. Descend slowly on to a lower saddle covered in loose scree, and then up the other side to the next summit. Be CAREFUL not to descend into the steep corrie that lies straight ahead. As you cross the saddle proper this drop will be very obvious on your right.

The top is an incredible wonderland of white quartzite, with the shattered rocks scattered about the summit in a confused jumble, giving the appearance of some alien planet. The Maumturks and neighbouring Twelve Bens are solid masses of quartzite. This whitened metamorphic rock glistens in the sunshine and often gives the impression of a thin layer of icing on the pointed peaks of the Bens,

The dipper will be found hopping about the stream-side rocks as it
plunges in and out of the fast-flowing currents in search of insects.

especially after rain. They are both ancient mountains laid down some
six hundred million years ago in pre-Cambrian times. Originally
sedimentary sands, they were later subjected to volcanic activity that
transformed the rock to crystalline quartzite.

From the top, the views northward along the spine of the
Maumturks are outstanding. Beyond them the faraway round-domed
Sheeffry Hills hold one in awe. Further to your right is the heath-clad
Joyce Country, running off to the similarly coated Partry mountains.
While away across the Inagh valley on your left, the craggy peaks of the
mighty Twelve Bens shoot up dramatically from the tree-smothered
shores of Lough Inagh.

(12) Climb up the slope on the other side of the saddle and make for
the un-named peak.

Along the way there is plenty of BELL HEATHER (*Erica cinerea*)
amongst the rocks, while on more exposed ground it is hard to avoid
standing on the many clumps of FIR CLUBMOSS (*Lycopodium selago*).
However, no matter how common it may appear here, you must still
remember its reduced distribution, so it should not be picked.

(13) On reaching the top you should find a small mound of stones.
From this, go slightly to the RIGHT into a dip and make for the next rise

Numerous delightful cascades pour from the rocky
summits in these regions.

visible ahead, going up its LEFT side. There is the outline of a rough footpath up along this left side, but be careful of the steep drop down on your left.

(14) Eventually you reach the top of the ridge just as it swings around to your left. Climbing up on to the ridge, follow it to your LEFT and climb gradually up to the peak of Cnoc Doire Bhó Riada (hill of the tame cow wood). You should be able to find the crude outline of a path up on the LEFT-hand side of this rising ridge.

As you cross the ridge, there is an impressively deep gorge down on your right. This was carved out by a giant glacier during the long Ice Age that covered much of these mountains for over two million years. Wearing down the mountain sides, it gouged out these steep-sided corries and carried the debris of rock for many miles. Many quartzite boulders ended up as far away as the Aran islands, having been deposited on the limestone terraces by the melting ice.

(15) From the top of Cnoc Doire Bhó Riada, start swinging around to the RIGHT, first descending into a small hollow and then gradually working your way up to a second rise. From the second rise, continue slightly to the RIGHT and up on to the summit of Binn Idir an Dhá Log (peak between two hollows).

(16) On reaching the top of Binn Idir an Dá Log, continue north-west, descending the steep slope until you reach a sheer drop. STOP. Below you is a mountain tarn or lake (see the illustration at the beginning of this walk).

Binn Idir an Dá Log (2307ft/703m) is the highest point of the Maumturks and there are excellent views up towards the top of the Inagh valley. From left to right are the waters of Kylemore Lough, Lough Fee and Killary Harbour. Above the latter is the tall dome of Mweelrea mountain, which marks the southern boundary of county Mayo.

(17) When you are able to look down on the tarn, go to the extreme RIGHT and slowly descend the scree-covered slope of loose rock and pebbles. DO NOT GO STRAIGHT DOWN THE CLIFF FACE.

The slope is steep and the scree of boulders and stones is loose so take your time and watch your footing. The inexperienced may find this descent rather trying but with good boots and your hands free, you will reach the bottom safely, to arrive beside the tarn's exiting stream.

(18) At the bottom of the incline a sheep-wire fence blocks the way. Do not climb over it, but go to the LEFT by going clockwise around the tarn until you meet another fence on the other side. Follow the fence up over the rocky ridge and then down on to the lowest part of the saddle where there are some ruptured black banks of peat. Stay close to the fence on your right.

This is the pass of Mám Ochóige, from which the tarn gets its name. The characteristic heath is beginning to return, so watch for the few birds that do occur in these parts such as the WHEATEAR (*Oenanthe oenanthe*) and SKYLARK (*Alauda arvensis*). You will also surely encounter the RAVEN (*Corvus corax*) as it soars over the cliffs emitting its lonesome croak. The raven is an early breeding bird and generally engages in its mating display as early as January.

(19) At the lowest part of the saddle, go sharply to your LEFT, descending the steep grassy slope. Further down, you reach a small stream which you follow down to the tarred road.

Along the way, there are several wet and soggy patches which support insect-eating SUNDEW (*Drosera rotundifolia*) and MARSH VIOLET (*Viola palustris*). Throughout the earlier part of summer there are also plenty of HEATH SPOTTED-ORCHID (*Dactylorhiza maculata*) pushing its spike of spotted pale-pink flowers up through the damp meadows. On either side, the drier ground continues up the hillsides coated in thick swards of bracken that turn a delightful russet brown in autumn and contrast sharply with the barren white peaks up above.

The stream eventually opens out into a clear stony brook, interspersed with several small pools and little falls, quite a delightful place to bathe your feet on the warmer summer days. Such immature mountain streams are usually low in nutrients and so have little in the way of insect life. However, you may still spot the DIPPER (*Cinclus*

cinclus), that delightful black bird of rivers and streams which has a characteristic white apron patch beneath its chin. Additionally, the bobbing yellow-bellied GREY WAGTAIL (*Motacilla cinerea*) flits about the rocks in mid-stream.

(20) When the stream reaches a bridge, climb up on to the tarred road and go to the LEFT. After 2ml/3.4km you arrive back at the car park (1).

Along the way, you pass several houses surrounded by small meadows. Very exposed and devoid of trees, save for a few fuchsia bushes, this area was once covered in woodland, as a glance down to the lake on your right will show you. This large body of water is Loch Leitheanach and there are several trees on its islands. These are remnants from a time when the drier meadows supported woods full of OAK, BIRCH, HOLLY and HAZEL. Now, a great sea of bog stretches across the valley and turf is cut. During drier summers, the harvested reeks of cut turf line the roadside as you make your way back to the start of the walk.

8 - Lackavrea Hill

NO TWO POINTS IN CONNEMARA offer the same perspective, so it is always invigorating to climb new peaks and enjoy the changing panorama over this wild landscape of water, bog, mountain and sea.

Its ruggedness is its magic and its saviour. The old tribes of Galway held sway here for centuries, against the invading forces of foreign lands. In the distant middle-ages there was surely none more remarkable then the legendary Grace O' Malley, Pirate Queen of the West. Climbing any of the high peaks about these quarters fires the imagination when pondering on the exploits of this remarkable lady. One such spot is Lackavrea Hill where one can look down on the wilderness where she lived and fought, as in the island fortress of Hen's Castle. Usually hidden from view it lies on the upper reaches of Lough Corrib and illustrates beautifully the difficulty an invading army would have had in attacking it. That is, if they found it first.

The fortress-like nature of the terrain that shielded Grace O Malley in times past, is as clearly visible today as it was then. Hopefully it too will protect it from the excess of modern commercialism and exploitation, insuring that the wild character of this charming country will be preserved intact.

WALK DESCRIPTION

LOCATION: Travelling on the Galway-Clifden road, take the R336 north from Maam Cross (the cross is 35km/22ml from Clifden). Continue north for 2km/1.2ml until you reach a lane on the RIGHT, at a bend. This should have a gate, with some timber fencing and a stepped stile, as well as a walking sign for the Western Way (Slí an Iarthar). There is limited parking here at the start, so park sensibly. Also be careful on this busy road, especially during the summer season.

TERRAIN: This is sheep farming country, so NO DOGS please.

As you drive up from Maam Cross, the high peaks of the Maumturk Mountains will be on your left while Lackavrea Hill will be on your right – the latter looking deceptively easy. Despite its lower altitude (396m) it still involves a steep climb, so not for the inexperienced. The ground can be very wet on the approach and even wetter on the exit, so wear good waterproof boots and gaiters.

LENGTH: 5ml/8km.

TIME: 4–5 hours.

EQUIPMENT: Back pack for refreshments and rain gear: Reliable waterproof, hiking boots with a good grip. Carrying a pair of wellingtons in the backpack for the homeward journey would be helpful, especially if it has been wet. Walking pole.

MAPS: OS Discovery Series numbers 38 and 45.

WHEN TO WALK: Not to be attempted during misty or foggy weather, or if there is a threat of low rain cloud descending on the mountain. You

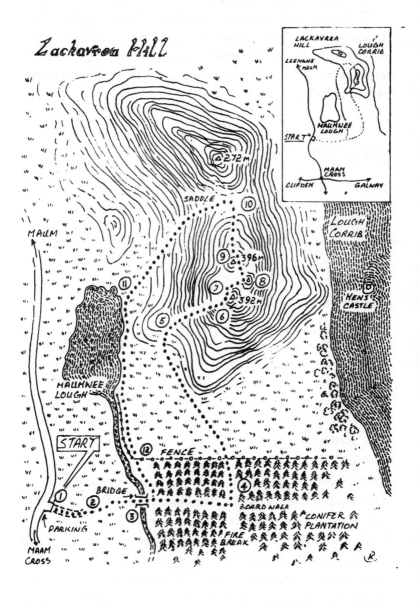

Zackavrea Hill

MAUM

LACKAVREA HILL
LOUGH CORRIB
LEENANE
MAUM
START
MAUMNEE LOUGH
MAAM CROSS
CLIFDEN
GALWAY

△ 272 M

SADDLE ⑩

LOUGH CORRIB

⑪

⑨ △ 396 M

⑦ ⑧

△ 392 M

⑤ ⑥

HENS CASTLE

MAUMNEE LOUGH

⑫ FENCE

START

BRIGE

① ②

③

④

BOARD WALK CONIFER PLANTATION

PARKING

FIRE BREAK

MAAM CROSS

need clear visibility when on top in order to locate a safe descent point. Remember you are on the Atlantic seaboard and there can be sudden weather changes. Obtain an up-to-date weather report before setting out.

WALK OUTLINE

(1) Having parked near the entrance lane, follow the rough track into the boggy terrain. As you walk, take notice of the high peak of Lackavrea Hill up to your left and assess the climbing potential for access to the top, the best route being at the southwest corner nearest to you.

(2) Shortly, the track peters out as it nears a wallking pole marker on a rise, after which the route follows sheets of plastic matting across the bog. This leads you down to a conifer plantation where a metal bridge takes you over the river and into the plantation.

The star sedge (top) and pale butterwort (bottom) are characteristic of the wet heath around Lackavrea.

The matting is essential due to the very wet nature of the terrain, but it is also indicative of the unique habitat type, which is 'Oceanic blanket-bog'. Depending on the time of year, a diverse collection of wild flowersand sedges can be encountered, thriving in the water-logged soil. In spring the ground is covered on all sides with the delightful red blooms of Lousewort (*Pedicularis palustris*), while in summer the yellow-flowered Tormentil (*Potentilla erecta*), the purple-flowered Heath Milkworth (*Polygala serpyllifolia*) adorn the heath.

(3) On crossing the bridge, follow the 'board-walk' on the other side across the very wet ground, as it leads you through a substantial opening or fire break in the forest. Follow this through the trees for about 15–20 minutes until another distinctive fire break cuts across the forest at right angles to the board walk.

(4) On reaching the intersecting fire break, leave the board walk and pass through the opening in the trees on your LEFT, where at the forest edge a dilapidated fence takes you out onto the open heath and clear views of Lackavrea Hill are visible. Maintain a STRAIGHT course heading for the mid point of the sloping ridge on the left-hand side of the Hill apex.

Initially the ground is very wet, but as you gain height it becomes drier, while better and better views begin to unfold. Over to your left is the start of the Maumturks, while on the right the waters of Lough Corrib begin to appear.

Lackavrea translates as the 'ragged rock', which is close to the truth. As you climb, numerous rocky protrusions are met, between which squelch the ragged sheets of wet heath. If it has been dry and you have a good grip on your boots, it is easier at times to walk along the exposed rock.

These lower slopes support a typical heathland flora. Wet and soft, the uncut turf beneath your feet is covered in a thick carpet of sedges. There are as many as seventy different types of sedge found throughout Ireland, several quite similar and thus hard to identify. However, the STAR SEDGE *(Carex echinata)* is recognisable, its seed heads forming distinctive star-shaped spike. Quite a common species, it is well-adapted to surviving in the mineral-deficient bog. In the shorter tufts of sedge, the pink-flowered PALE BUTTERWORT *(pinguicula lusitanica)* can be found. This feeds on insects by curling its short sticky leaves around its trapped victims and then secreting digestive juices to dissolve the body. Nitrogen and other essential minerals are then absorbed for the plant's metabolic processes.

(5) On reaching the top of the approach ridge – when you can see the upper end of the Maumturk Mountains – begin to swing to the RIGHT

and work your way up the rocky and steep slope. Use your common sense to pick the best route until the top is reached.

Pausing now and then to get one's 'second wind' and take in the views, the lake-studded landscape of south Connemara and the distant sea of Galway Bay are quite stunning with, at times, the water of a thousand pools shimmering in the bright sunlight.

(6) On reaching the top of the incline you arrive onto an open plateau of rocks and soggy peat pools. Here swing to the LEFT and head for the first peak identified by a pile of stones, which is about 100m away and slightly higher up.

(7) On reaching the first pile of stones (392m) a second pile becomes visible over to your RIGHT. Make for this by going diagonally to your RIGHT across the boggy and rocky terrain.

From the top there are fine views visible all around. To the right the island studded waters of Lough Corrib; behind, the lake-studded bogs of Connemara. Looking south towards Maam Cross the expanse of water logged bog leads towards the culturally rich and Irish speaking region of Gorumna Island and Carraroe, then ultimately south to Galway Bay. Over on your left are the fine quartzite peaks of the Maumturks, while down below on your right is the upper reach of the delightful Lough Corrib with the island fortress of Hen's Castle in the centre. Beyond Lough Corrib lies Lough Mask with its attendant Partry and Sheffry Hills skirting it to the west.

The white flower heads of sanicle will be found growing up through the oak-leaf-smothered woodland floor in early summer.

Looking to the right, the valleys below look impressive

with their sparkling sheets of water and must have looked even more so when they were covered in oak forest three hundred years ago. Then the countryside teemed with a wealth of wildlife that today is hard even to imagine. Great herds of red deer roamed the hills, wolves, wild boar, squirrels, and pine martens filled the forests, golden eagles soared over the Twelve Bens, seals followed the salmon into the freshwater lakes, while large numbers of whales filled the coastal waters.

(8) On reaching the second pile of stones the true peak is visible ahead, again marked by a small pile of stones and near some wire fencing. Make STRAIGHT for this, keeping the fence on your right.

Keep an eye out for the majestic peregrine falcon about the high cliffs.

But first, from this peak there is an excellent view down onto Castlekirke, or Hens Castle. This castle is named in honour of the legendary Grace O' Malley, the sixteenth-century 'Pirate Queen'. She was a daring, fearless and shrewd leader that controlled much of the West of Ireland during those turbulent times – both on land and sea. She raided wealthy merchant ships and united many of the warring clans of the area to become their unquestioned leader. However she was perpetually hounded by the sadistic and degenerate Bingham, Queen Elizabeth's General in Ireland. Her most famous exploit was her meeting with Queen Elizabeth in 1593. Though a named outlaw in the eyes of the English, she sailed up the Thames and was granted an audience. She so charmed the monarch that she had her territories restored. But in Ireland Bingham was having none of it and persecuted her to the very last.

Being a woman she was disliked by the Irish authorities and her memory was obliterated from all Irish records. The only records that survived were those of the English. Today the legends of this incredible Irish character are beginning to be recognised and her place in the annals of Irish history properly restored.

(9) On reaching the true peak (396m), surrounded by pools of liquid turf, the hill quickly drops down the other side and onto a lower ridge or saddle. Descend from the peak carefully and cross the saddle until the lowest point is reached, about mid-way across.

From the summit point the adjacent Maumwee Lough is clearly seen and there are fine views northwards up the distant valley of 'Joyce's river', and on into the delightful Joyce's Country, at the very head of which is the village of Leenane and Killary Harbour.

(10) On reaching the mid-point of the saddle, proceed until you can see a clear way down onto the boggy heath below on the LEFT. Then descend zig-zag fashion and carefully work your way back towards the near shore of Maumwee Lough. Lower down the ground again becomes very wet and in summer the grass will be very high, therefore you need to tread carefully and take your time. Use your trekking pole to indicate and avoid any gullies or depressions hidden in the high grass.

The heath on this side of Maumwee Lough is relatively undisturbed, save for a few ponies. As a result the moth ecology is excellent, with some of the brown coloured ones such as the Oak eggar moth (*Lasiocampa quercus*) quite noticeable.

On your left, the high boney ridge of Lackavrea rises up in a series of punctured cliffs. Around these cliffs you may be lucky enough to hear the haunting scream of the PEREGRINE FALCON *(Falco peregrinus)*, a bird that came very close to extinction due to excessive use of pesticides such as DDT, but is now making a gradual comeback. This pesticide does not break down easily; instead it accumulates in food chains, becoming concentrated at the top and causing the death of those animals at this level of the food chain.

(11) On reaching the lough margin follow the shoreline down to its exit stream, near some wire fencing.

Out on the lough, being safe from grazing, the islands are covered in several varieties of stunted trees, such as oak, birch and holly. These are indicative of the natural vegetation that would have existed here as little as four hundred years ago. They also contain the typical woodland vegetation – in spring PRIMROSE *(Primula vulgaris)* and COMMON DOG-VIOLET *(Viola riviniana)* appear, while later in the summer months the shade-tolerant WOOD SANICLE *(Sanicula europea)*, BUGLE *(Ajuga reptans)* and MALE-FERN *(Dryopteris felixmas)* grow.

On the water, few birds are evident other than the diving SHAGS *(Phalacrocorax aristotelis)* and long-legged GREY HERONS *(Ardea cinerea)*. Both birds are indicative of a clean healthy lough that is well-stocked with fish.

(12) On reaching the exit stream keep the fence on your right and follow it STRAIGHT down to a corner, next to the forest plantation. There, cross the wire carefully and follow the strip of soggy bog, down between the stream and the trees, until you shortly reach the metal bridge again.

(3) You are now back at the outward point (3) so go to the RIGHT, over the bridge and back to the start.

9 – Killary Harbour

KILLARY HARBOUR IS A REMARKABLE SINUOUS STRETCH of water that winds its way in between the fastnesses of the high mountains, clearly delineating the boundary between north Connemara and south Mayo. A natural fjord-like drowned valley, all of 10ml/16km in length, it is the most beautiful of the sea inlets on the western seaboard. Mighty mountains soar up from the deep grey-blue waters, their curved and cliff-edged ridges overlapping one in front of another as they run in serried folds towards the distant sea.

Guarding the fjord mouth is the west's highest mountain, Mweelrea. Standing bold and defiant, Mweelrea rises abruptly from the watery depths to run uninterrupted in steep-sheeted blankets of heath towards the lofty summit. Great slabs of shattered and time-worn rock litter the upper slopes to scrape at rolling clouds setting them crown-like around its lofty peak. Down from the dizzy heights waterfall and torrent run in deep-veined channels through the folds of green-skinned heath, cutting deeply into its contours like veins on a torso.

In the midst of the mountains yet surrounded by the salty tang of sea air, a calmness reaches one from across the wide stretches of water. Truly this is the finest of all drowned, glaciated valleys in Ireland and a wondrous place to walk and explore.

WALK DESCRIPTION

LOCATION: The walk starts at Rosroe pier at the mouth of Killary Harbour. Travel 4.5ml/7km from the village of Leenane on the Leenane–Letterfrack road (the N59) and take the RIGHT turn-off for Tully Cross (sign-posted). Travel for another 3ml/4.8km, passing by the shores of Lough Fee, and go RIGHT at the next Y-junction with signs for Rosroe pier and Killary Salmon Farm. Continue along this road for another 2ml/3km to reach the pier, where you can park, ignoring any left turns.

TERRAIN: A moderate circular walk. The outward route follows a well-defined, but muddy and rock-strewn track, and returns by a less distinct but traversible track. This is extensive sheep-farming country, thus NO DOGS.

FEATURES: Spectacular views of the fjord and mountain masses; glacial features; heathland plants and birds; pre-famine remains.

LENGTH: 6ml/9.6km.

TIME: 3 hours.

EQUIPMENT: Waterproof walking boots are desirable. A walking stick would be helpful.

WHEN TO WALK: Any time of the year.

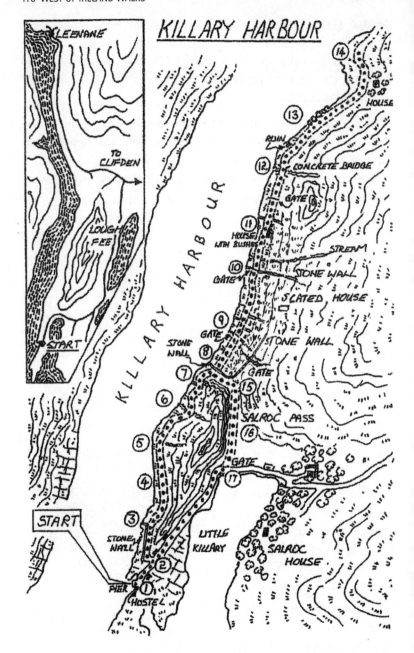

KILLARY HARBOUR

LEENANE

TO CLIFDEN

LOUGH FEE

START

KILLARY HARBOUR

HOUSE

RUIN

CONCRETE BRIDGE

GATE

HOUSE WITH BUSHES

STREAM

STONE WALL

SLATED HOUSE

GATE

STONE WALL

GATE

STONG WALL

GATE

SALROC PASS

GATE

START

STONE WALL

LITTLE KILLARY

SALROC HOUSE

PIER

HOSTEL

WALK OUTLINE

(1) Having parked at the pier, walk back UP along the approach road for about a hundred metres and take a LEFT turn on to a lane beside the first house on the left.

(2) Follow this old lane as it spirals up into the rocky heathland and then swings to the RIGHT along the side of a stone wall. Keep the wall on your left and follow it to its end.

There are excellent views over the mouth of the fjord and to the nearby ocean, speckled with many large and small islands. At the mouth of the fjord is Inis Bearna (gap island), once the home of Seán Mac Conmara, the Irish folk poet. Born in the 1770s, he lived through the famine years of 1845-47, writing many moving songs. However, he is best known for his famous song which commemorates the drowning of his son.

Further out to sea are the larger islands of Inishbofin on the left, Inishturk in the middle and Clare Island to the right.

(3) When the wall ends, the track continues STRAIGHT on, following the outline of the fjord as it meanders inland.

From here, there are excellent views down to the shoreline and across to the impressive massif of Mweelrea as it soars upwards from shore to summit through a staggering 2688ft/815m.

This ancient bony mountain has roots buried deep in the past, the base rock being of sedimentary grits and sandstone laid down in ancient seas sometime between four hundred to six hundred

The yellow-petalled common tormentil is characteristic of the rocky heath.

million years ago. Since then, the bedrock of Mweelrea and the surrounding mountains have been folded, lifted, exposed to volcanic activity and eroded by time to produce their present shape.

(4) As you walk along the stony track, the low vegetation appears stunted and sparse with just a few yellow-petalled COMMON TORMENTIL (*Potentilla erecta*) and in wetter callows some RUSH (*Juncus*) and SEDGE (*Carex*).

However, in former times, with the addition of seaweed to the soil, these barren hills were able to produce ample supplies of food. Looking across the fjord again at the mountain base, you should be able to spot, within the scant remains of small fields, a series of parallel lines that run perpendicularly to the shore. These are the disused potato ridges of a small community of people who clung to life here on the edge of this almost inaccessible stretch of heath. Forced by oppression to come here during the eighteenth century, these people managed to build a crude settlement on the steep slopes, making their small fields from a mixture of seaweed and impoverished soil on which they grew their staple diet of potatoes. Land evictions and the horrific famine of 1845 finally obliterated the greater part of the population here.

(5) The track swings around a gentle curve with views down on to the seaweed-covered rocks beneath. Lobster-pot floats bob up and down along the shoreline, their anchor lines disappearing into the shadowy depths. The fjord is unique as it retains an average depth of 80ft/26m throughout its length, and is actually shallower at its seaward end. Part of a major fault line in the surrounding mountain masses, this fjord became an ancient V-shaped river valley. However, during the last great Ice Age, a glacier cut its way downwards, broadening and deepening the valley into a U-shape. Subsequently the valley was drowned by the rise in sea levels that occurred at the end of the Ice Age roughly eight thousand years ago, giving us the present spectacular fjord.

(6) Presently the track is crossed by a small stream, before it climbs up over a small rise.

The common sandpiper may be found flying over
the water's edge, emitting its shrill cry.

From the top of the rise, views along the length of the fjord open up, with the peak of Bucán mountain towering upwards. Bucán marks the end of the Maumturk mountain range, behind which hides the small village of Leenane and the fjord's upper end.

Large rafts on the water tend to marr the wonderful views. These are salmon-rearing cages and mussel beds, both part of a new initiative to create employment in the region. Mussel beds are generally clean and do not need much care-taking. However, salmon cages are highly polluting and should not be sited in such an enclosed body of water as the dispersal of the large amount of organic waste fed to and produced by the fish is inhibited. But salmon are also very dependent on clean healthy water, so as a part of the region's economy they will require high environmental standards to be maintained. With luck, this may mean that less sensitive developments are prevented, such as excessive holiday home developments with their associated domestic effluent, agricultural run-off or coastal pollution like oil or chemical spillage. They are also preferable to the environmental catastrophe that could result from the shadow that hangs over these mountains and the waters of Killary fjord: gold has been discovered in the large stretch of mountains from Killary Harbour to Clew Bay. If mining operations are allowed to proceed, the consequence for the environment will be devastating as excessive chemical run-off enters the water courses that empty into Killary Harbour. This will wipe out all life in this unpolluted region. Ironically then, these unsightly cages may yet prove to be a valuable argument in the preservation of the healthy ecology of the fjord.

(7) Later, another small stream is crossed and the track climbs up over another low rise before dipping down towards the stone-walled fields beyond.

In the wetter pockets of the stream a few insect-eating COMMON BUTTERWORT (*Pinguicula vulgaris*) and SUNDEW (*Drosera rotundifolia*) may be found. The violet flower heads of the butterwort are quite noticeable in May and June, while the sticky hairy leaves of the sundew appear throughout summer. Occasionally, the delicate strands of pink-flowered BOG PIMPERNEL (*Anagallis tenella*) can also be spotted on the turfbanks throughout the summer months. Among the low heather and the odd clump of bracken fern, watch for the WHEATEAR (*Oenanthe oenanthe*), identifiable by its black-and-white tail. The wheatear is not a very musical bird, but you may hear the piping notes of the COMMON SANDPIPER (*Actitis hypoleucos*) along the rocky shoreline below.

(8) When you reach a stone wall with a stile cross it with care. 100m afterwards another stream flows under the grass-covered track. NOTE: you must return to this point to complete the circular route.

A mottled pattern of encrusting lichens colours the stones of the wall in pale shades of pink, blue-grey and white, not unlike countries on a map. Lichens are treated indifferently by some, but their primitive nature means that they are totally dependent on the air for all their material needs. Thus they are excellent indicators of air quality as they are unable to tolerate the presence of pollutants like sulphur dioxide. A total absence of lichens is a sure sign that the air is badly polluted. So breathe deeply here!

(9) Presently you reach a gully and a stone wall with a gap, pass through and continue to follow the track STRAIGHT ahead.

(10) Later a number of abandoned houses are visible on your right and you pass through a gap in a stone wall.

Down to the left, better-quality fields slide down the steep slope to the waters below. On some the ribbed pattern of old potato drills indicates their former use. The drills were raised to facilitate good drainage for this tuberous crop. Potatoes are actually swollen underground stems rather than roots, so they like dry conditions. Excessive wetness promotes the growth of fungal attacks, such as POTATO BLIGHT (*Phytophtora infestans*). It was a succession of exceedingly damp and wet summers that led to the final collapse of the crop in 1845, the blight causing the tubers to rot in the ground and so precipitating the horrific famine.

(11) Shortly afterwards, you reach an abandoned low cottage with bushes on the right-hand side of the track, after which there is an open gap (can occasionally have a gate). Pass through the gap and continue STRAIGHT.

Looking across the fjord, you can discern the large glaciated coombe on Mweelrea's north-eastern side. A large glacier gouged it out as it worked its way down to enter the fjord beneath the high peak of Ben Gorm. The entry point was around the bend in the fjord up ahead.

(12) Later on the track crosses over a concrete bridge beneath which a stream pours in small waterfalls and cascades. At the other side of the bridge there is a metal gate, please re-close after you.

The vegetation here is still sparse, save for a few stunted HAWTHORN (*Crataegus*) bushes and ASH (*Fraximus*) trees. After a good summer, large flocks of STARLING (*Sturnus vulgaris*) comb through the fields, while out on the water the occasional SHAG (*Phalacrocorax aristotelis*) can be seen as it flies through the fjord. Shags may be hard to spot because of their black colouring and because they spend much time underwater hunting for fish. The most that one can see of them on re-emerging is their long thin neck, as the bulk of their body remains below the surface.

(13) Presently you reach another gate with a stone-built boat house and pier below on the left. About here you come very close to the water's edge.

Brown seaweeds coat the rocks, confirming that we are still beside the sea. Near the shoreline several trees have managed to escape the depredations of humans and quite a good mix of species is evident in the small copse. OAK, ASH, HAZEL, MOUNTAIN ASH, HAWTHORN, SALLY, SILVER BIRCH and HOLLY are all here. They are native species and are all that remains of the great forests that once cloaked this wilderness.

(14) Continue to follow the track past a house, sensitively screened by the trees on your right, where you encounter another gate. Having re-closed the gate, follow the track up and out on to a conspicuous promontory. Here the route ENDS and you must return to point (8) in order to complete the walk.

From this vantage point, you can gaze up the remaining section of the fjord and see some of the distant houses of the village of Leenane. It was in 1903 that the British naval fleet entered this fjord with none other than King Edward VII and Queen Alexander on board. They docked here and went on a sightseeing tour of the region and were entertained in the nearby Kylemore Abbey.

(8) On returning to the stone wall with the stepped stile, cross over the wall and go uphill to the LEFT, following a rough path. Keep the stone wall on your left until it comes to an end half-way up the hill.

The red admiral is a common coastal butterfly. Arriving from the Mediterranean region in spring, it quickly breeds to produce native offspring.

Up on your right the heath rises sharply and the vegetation is of the blanket bog type, predominantly PURPLE MOOR-GRASS *(Molinia caerulea)* and a variety of SEDGES. However, the different months throw out their many coloured blossoms. On the drier outcrops HEATHER *(Erica)* glows purple in the month of September, the spiky yellow flower heads of the BOG ASPHODEL *(Narthecium ossifragum)* appear in August, while the white tufts of COMMON COTTON GRASS *(Eriophorum angustifolium)* flutter on the wetter parts of the moor in May and June.

(15) On reaching the end of the stone wall, a sheep wire fence continues up the hill, gradually leading to the RIGHT, up into a deep ravine. Keep the fence on your left and follow the rough, rocky trail up into the ravine. Parts of this are rather difficult so tread slowly and with care.

On the left-hand side of the ravine, waves of heath pour down on to the rough track while the opposite side is shattered cliff, half-covered with scree. This curious ravine is known as Salroc Pass and leads down into Little Killary, which was a safe harbour used by smugglers in days past. The goods once landed were carried by pack-horse up through Salroc Pass and then transported inland along the old route you have just walked.

(16) Having reached the top of the pass, descend the other side to locate a gate on the roadside. As you descend, the craggy cliffs open out and give fine views across the harbour of Little Killary, with the wooded grounds of Salroc House over on the left.

Salroc House is the former residence of the landlords of the area, the Millers, who were granted all the lands hereabouts following the Cromwellian conquests of the seventeenth century. Later, in the nineteenth century, Alexander Thompson married into the family and began evicting many of the tenants from the estate, replacing them with sheep. He was one of the first pre-famine landlords to do so. This depopulated the lands around Killary, and the results are still evident today. However, Thompson also planted the many BEECH trees which now adorn this picturesque bay and make it unique in this otherwise treeless wilderness. With time, he and later generations became more sympathetic to the plight of their tenants and during the famine years fed and cared for many. The Thompson's daughter, in particular, cared deeply for the tenants, helping many, and providing them with employment. However, she still defended her legal rights, for example in the family's fisheries in the surrounding waters, and would swim the creek in order to catch poachers, showing no mercy in dealing with offenders.

(17) At the bottom of the grassy hill a wooden but delicate gate leads on to the tarred road. Open it carefully, walk on to the road and go to the RIGHT, following the delightful stretch of coast road back to the pier and the car (1).

Mayo

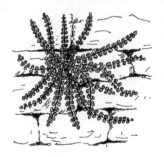

10 – Cong

THE WILDS OF WESTERN IRELAND are open and exposed, a terrain that
at times can become quite tedious and rough for walking, especially
when the weather turns foul and the rain and damp play upon one's
patience. So it is enjoyable to explore a walk that gives a sense of shelter
and is not totally dependent on wide open spaces and their stunning
vistas. Such is the appeal of the wooded demesne of Ashford Castle on
the northern shore of the regal Lough Corrib. Old paths weave their
way through the sylvan countryside of shady glades, river, lake and
tree-lined meadows, where curiosities of both a human and natural

order abound. It also hides a romantic story of undying love complete with fairytale castle, towers, caves and secret places.

Situated just over the Mayo border and on the thin isthmus between Lough Mask and Lough Corrib, Cong guards the north-eastern entrance to Connemara. It is an enchanted landscape that does not sit comfortably within the general concept of the Connemara experience. However, such a disparity clearly illustrates the divide between the ruling classes of the nineteenth century and their tenants. Here on the shores of Lough Corrib is a beautiful old estate. Stunning, but also sad when one realises the wealth that was concentrated in the hands of the few ruling families of the time, while around the high-walled estates the tenants suffered unimaginable hardship. It is hard to introduce Ireland's west without first having to confront the nightmare of its recent past. But first, a walk through the woods at Cong will tell one side of the story.

WALK DESCRIPTION

LOCATION: The walk begins and ends in the picturesque village of Cong. Park in the car park opposite the ruined Cong Abbey.

TERRAIN: A delightful casual and circular walk along the many wooded paths, with a short stretch of tarred road. It is an ideal walk for those with children as it is full of surprises. However, it can be enjoyed by all and is perfect for those overcast days when the mountains are inaccessible, or totally invisible.

FEATURES: Cong Abbey; Ashford Castle; caves; tunnel; dry canal; deciduous and coniferous woods with related flora and fauna; riverside, lakeshore and woodland paths; panoramic views across Lough Corrib; a short OPTION is available to visit an old viewing tower.

LENGTH: 5.5ml/9km. The OPTION is 0.5ml/0.8km extra.

TIME: 3 hrs. The OPTION is 0.5 hrs extra.

CONG

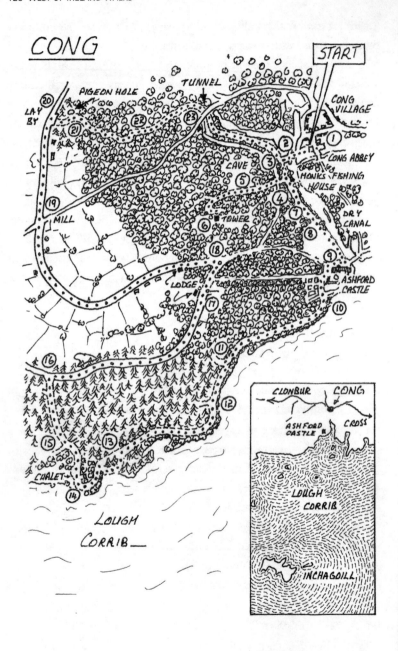

EQUIPMENT: Comfortable walking shoes but wellingtons are more appropriate if it is wet. Bring a flashlamp for the caves. NOTE an admission fee may be payable to enter the castle grounds at point (4).

WHEN TO WALK: Suitable at any time of the year.

WALK OUTLINE

(1) From the car park, cross the road and go STRAIGHT through the abbey ruins. Exit through the rear cloister and on to the lawn lined with yew trees. Maintain a STRAIGHT course and follow the path to the river.

The Royal Abbey of Cong reflects the turbulent and intriguing history of the region over the last thousand years. Originally the monastic site of the seventh-century St Fechín, it later became the dominion of the kings of Connacht when, in 1134, Turlough O' Connor, King of Connacht and High King of Ireland, built the present edifice for the canons regular of the Order of St Augustine. It was here that Rory O'Connor, Ireland's last High King, died in 1198, having failed to prevent the Norman invasions of the twelfth century. The abbey was destroyed and rebuilt several times, surviving through centuries of invasion and religious persecution, such as the dark penal days of King Henry VIII in the sixteenth century. Despite the centuries of turmoil the

Oak

Holm oak

Ash

Lime

Beech

Sycamore

abbey survived and the last recorded abbot died in 1829.

(2) At the end of the line of yew trees, cross the rustic footbridge, go through the stone arch and follow the path as it winds through the trees. This leads you past the monks' fishing house before crossing another footbridge and going beneath a second stone arch into Cong Wood.

The rivers are unusual in that they are the freshly risen waters of Lough Mask. Having flowed underground for several miles through the limestone base of the region, the river re-emerges in the village of Cong at the 'Rising of the Waters' and then flows on to Lough Corrib. It was around here and in the abbey that many scenes from the 1951 film *The Quiet Man* were shot.

Both arched gateways have a head carved on their keystone. The first is reputed to be the head of the last abbot of the abbey, Abbot Prendergast; the second is that of Rory O'Connor, the last High King of Ireland.

The delightful monks' fishing house is accessible via another flagged footbridge. This little ruined house has a hole in the floor through which the occupants of the abbey used to catch fish. A net was lowered through the hole into the river and this was connected to a bell in the abbey. When a fish was caught in the net, the bell rang, alerting the monks to their catch.

(3) On passing through the second arch into Cong Wood, you immediately come to a T-junction. Go LEFT and follow the rather muddy riverside path through the dark tunnel of trees until you come to an obvious junction at an iron gate.

The conifer trees are choked with the thickets of evergreen LAUREL, preventing a more luxurious ground vegetation from growing. However, anything that can outgrow the choking thicket survives remarkably well. These woods are part of the Ashford Castle estate and were extensively planted with an impressive collection of foreign species of trees. Along the path watch for the giant CALIFORNIAN REDWOODS, MONTEREY PINE as well as LODGE POLE PINE.

The moorhen can be seen quite regularly as it feeds on riverside vegetation. It may be recognised by its black appearance, red beak, and its bobbing gait as it moves through the water.

Throughout the estate you should also see LIME, HOLM OAK, PLANE, ATLANTIC and RED CEDARS, GOLDEN CYPRESS, FIG, HORNBEAM, WALNUT, and MONKEY PUZZLE, as well as the common species of HORSE CHESTNUT, MAPLE, OAK and BEECH. A visit to the Japanese gardens of the castle will reward the more enthusiastic tree-lover.

(4) At the Y-junction, one arm of which has an iron gate, the OPTION becomes available. If you are not taking this, go to the LEFT, passing through the gateway and follow the text from point (7).

OPTION

Do not go through the gate but take the RIGHT turn, and follow the path to a four-cross track. Keep going STRAIGHT across the junction and follow the rather overgrown path through the woods.

(5) After about fifty metres, watch for a sign-posted path with a seat and some railings branching into the trees on the RIGHT, and leading into the grotto of Teach Aille (house of the cliff). On returning from the grotto to the original path, go to the RIGHT and regain your original course.

The path takes you into a small cavern beneath a dark cliff where some slippery steps lead down into a deep hollow. During rainy weather an underground river passes through the cave. This is part of the extensive network of underground rivers that seep through the porous bedrock of limestone in this area. In essence it is Lough Mask seeping through the ground into Lough Corrib since no overground river connects these two large and neighbouring lakes. The grotto is cool throughout the year and so was used for storing butter and as a source of fresh water by the monks of the abbey.

The beauty of Ashford Castle is nicely set off by the large
circular fountain in the rear gardens.

(6) Further up, you come to a rough Y-junction. Here, go to the LEFT and as you turn around the bend keep a watchful eye out for the tall stone tower hidden in the trees on your RIGHT. It is about two hundred metres to a small rough path that leads you into the tower.

Joyce's Tower, as this tower is known, was built by the first member of the Guinness family to live on the Ashford estate, Sir Benjamin Lee Guinness. Seventy-nine steps lead to the lookout where an inscription gives the date of construction as 1864, so this landlord was at least providing employment for his tenants in the dark years following the famine. The tower commands excellent views of the woodlands, where JAYS (*Garrulus glandarius*) and WOODPIGEONS (*Columba palumbus*) can be seen. On a clear day, you can see the distant Partry mountains to the north-west and nearby Lough Corrib to the south. Sadly, this is now closed off and inaccessible.

(4) Leaving the tower behind, return to the riverside path by the same route and go to the RIGHT, through the iron gate.

(7) Continue following the riverside path through the woods to arrive on the wide lawns running up to Ashford Castle.

The vegetation along the river is wild and so supports a fine collection of native plant life. Water-loving ALDER TREES (*Alnus glutinosa*) stabilise the river banks. YELLOW WATER-LILIES (*Nuphar lutea*), BULRUSH (*Typha latifolia*) and BOGBEAN (*Menyanthes trifoliata*) grow in rich thickets, while the string-like strands of CROWFOOT (*Ranunculus aquatilis*) waver in the fast-flowing currents. MALLARD (*Anas platyrhynchos*), MOORHEN (*Gallinula chloropus*) and GREY HERON (*Ardea cinerea*) roam the rivers freely and if your luck is in you may even surprise the elusive PINE MARTEN (*Martes martes*), scurrying through the branches of the CALIFORNIAN REDWOODS. The pine marten is an extremely rare mammal found in a few undisturbed areas of Ireland. Its survival can be guaranteed only by retaining its last few habitats in as wild and natural a state as possible. Long live the weeds!

(8) On arriving at the castle lawns, continue STRAIGHT along the riverbank to pass underneath the stone arch and into the forecourt of the castle.

NOTE: There may be an attendant and an admission fee at the gate. Also, if for any reason the gate is closed go to the RIGHT along the tarred road, passing up by the heli-pad. Shortly after, take the first LEFT turn, towards another large, chain-locked gate. Standing in front of the gate, take note of and follow the muddy path for a few metres into the trees on the RIGHT. Within, you should find a moated foot-bridge leading into the gardens. Failing that, keep with the woodland path until you find the steps that lead down to the gardens, and so work your way back to point (10).

As you approach the arched castle entrance, look across to the other side of the river where you should see one of the locks of the dry canal! Not very obvious at first as it looks like another stream entering a river, to see it more clearly you may have to cross on to the castle bridge.

After the horrific famine of 1845-47, it was decided to build a canal between Lough Mask and Lough Corrib, both as an economic investment and to provide useful employment. The workers carved and dug for five years but when it came to opening the lock gates, the water soon vanished as it leaked through the porous limestone bedrock. The engineers had completely overlooked the nature of the ground on which the canal was built, so the waters never reached Cong and the project ended in total failure.

(9) On arriving at the front of the castle, go to the RIGHT. Walk past the castle's front door and then swing LEFT around the castle to enter the majestic rear gardens.

The original castle was built in 1228 by the Anglo-Norman conquerors, the de Burgos. They had defeated the High King, Rory O'Connor of Cong Abbey, and consequently took possession of large tracts of western Ireland. However, the present edifice has its origins in the eighteenth century when the Oranmore and Browne families built their shooting lodge here. This was sold by the Encumbered Estates Court in 1855 to Sir Benjamin Lee Guinness, head of the brewery giant. Sir Benjamin was quick to improve the lot of his poverty-stricken tenants, employing many in improving the estate, while the shooting lodge was remodelled in the style of a French chateau. The chateau still forms the central core of the present Victorian baronial pile and this part is recognisable by its high gabled roofs.

In 1868 the estate passed to Sir Benjamin's son Arthur, first and last Lord Ardilaun and MP for Dublin. Lord Ardilaun became infatuated with Olive Hedges Eyre White, the daughter of the Third Earl of Bantry, marrying her in 1869 when she was only nineteen years old. He sold out his share in the brewery to his younger brother for a fortune and the couple spent much of the rest of their childless lives beautifying and developing Ashford. They added the huge and romantic east and west castellated wings, the castellated six-arched bridge across the river, as well as the terraced gardens. They are also responsible for the many coats of arms, family mottos, giant 'As' (for Ardilaun) and barons' coronets that adorn the various architectural features. They also added substantially to the vast collection of trees found throughout the estate.

On Lord Ardilaun's death the estate passed to his brother Lord Iveagh, who gave it to his son Ernest Guinness. Ernest later gave the estate as a gift to the Irish people and so it came under the control of the Forestry Department. They leased it to a Noel Huggard who converted it into an hotel. In 1970 the world-renowned hotel was acquired by John Mulcahy and an additional mock-castellated wing added to its eastern side. Today it is in the hands of a business consortium that includes the well-known Irish businessmen Michael Smurfit and Tony O' Reilly.

(10) Entering the rear gardens, with their delightful fountain, take a RIGHT and then an immediate LEFT which leads you down past the terraced gardens to a crossroads. Keep STRAIGHT across the junction and follow the shoreline path.

Ahead, the route wanders by the tree-lined shore of island-studded Lough Corrib. They say that it has as many islands as there are days in the year, and some are remarkably beautiful as well as containing artifacts of enormous architectural importance. During the sixth century, when Christianity was spreading across Ireland, it was safer for holy men to dwell on an island than on the mainland to avoid the tumultuous times and the marauding packs of wolves. As a result, many religious sites occur on islands. Inchagoill (island of the stranger), in particular, holds the fifth-century Teampall Phádraic, a church that dates from the time of St Patrick (mid-fifth century). Not far from the church stands the Lia Lugnaedon Mac Limenuch (the stone of Lugna), who, it is thought, was the nephew and navigator of St Patrick. This 2.5ft/76cm obelisk has a number of Roman characters etched into it. This is believed to be the oldest Christian inscription in Europe outside the catacombs.

(11) The path arrives at a Y-junction with a black-and-yellow-coloured iron barrier. Take the LEFT fork here, passing through the iron barrier, and follow the shoreline path that leads through the trees along the 'Chalet Walk'.

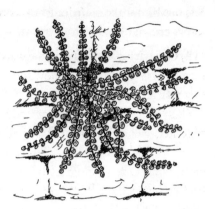

Less tamed, the chalet walk presents a good cross-section of wildlife. There are plenty of chances to see different butterflies, songbirds and wild

The black wiry stems and delicate green blades of the maidenhair spleenwort make it easily distinguishable.

flowers. There is also a good variety of trees overhead with OAK, ASH, BEECH, CHESTNUT, SPANISH CHESTNUT and SYCAMORE providing plenty of autumn colour. Also in autumn, you may notice strange black tar spots on some sycamore leaves. This is in fact a fungus unique to the sycamore.

(12) Presently you come to a rough Y-junction in the path, near a clearing in some conifer trees. Keep to the LEFT.

Remnants of former garden plants survive throughout the now wild woodland. Along the path, watch for RHODODENDRON as well as thickets of BAMBOO, a species of grass that grows to an enormous size.

(13) Nearing some conifer trees on your LEFT, watch for and take a short detour down to the lakeshore. At the lakeshore, cross the rough beach and find the path that leads you back into the woods. In the woods, watch for the RIGHT turn-off with timber railings that takes you back UP to the main path again. (This detour is easy to miss; if you do so just proceed on to point (14) on the map, about a hundred metres ahead.)

Across the lough, some of the many islands can be seen disappearing into the distant silver horizon stretching south towards Galway city.

You may also see many fishing boats on the lough as it is world-famous for its brown trout.

(14) On arriving at the chalet, the walk continues around the bend and through a large car park. Follow the exit road up to a +-junction. But first take an exploratory rest.

This is the viewpoint where Lady and Lord Ardilaun used to sit together, gazing at the spectacular sunsets across the panoramic views of Lough Corrib and towards the distant Maumturk mountains. One evening, Lady Ardilaun arrived at the viewpoint to find to her delight that Arthur had built the wooden chalet as a surprise for her birthday. Many an evening was spent together here and she delighted in bringing her friends to tea and to view the sunsets. A fine limestone fireplace stands inside the chalet and bears the date of construction, 1908.

Sadly, Lord Ardilaun was to die within seven years and Olive was to become a heartbroken and very lonely woman. To show her undying affection for him and her own great loss she had the nearby limestone obelisk erected. This gives plenty of information on Lord Ardilaun and is well worth reading. The various inscriptions detail his life as an MP and also give some details about Olive – she was the third daughter of the Third Earl of Bantry and Jane Herbert (of Muckross House, Killarney). It also bears a heart-rending inscription in French of how Olive suffered her loss: 'Rien ne m'est plus, plus ne m'est rien', which when translated, means roughly, 'I don't have anything anymore, nothing means anything to me anymore.'

Lord Ardilaun was an active MP for Dublin and showed a deep concern for the people of the city. Today, his statue stands in St Stephen's Green as he was responsible for its transformation from a drab enclosed square into a charming and popular park.

(15) Having followed the tarred road up from the car park and past some picnic tables, you shortly arrive at a +-junction. Maintain a STRAIGHT course, following the better tarred road.

(16) The road arrives at an open gate with a cattle grid and exits on to a T-junction. Go to the RIGHT and follow the road for the next 0.5ml/0.8km.

The quiet roadway ahead is overhung with coniferous trees while the roadside margins are thick with common weeds and associated insects. Watch for FRITILLARY and TORTOISESHELL butterflies as they alight on NETTLE (*Utrica dioica*), BRACKEN FERN (*Pteridium aquilinum*), BURDOCK (*Arctiun minus*) and HOGWEED (*Heracleum sphondylium*) – the latter is a native plant and not to be confused with the distasteful GIANT HOGWEED (*Heracleum mantegazzianum*), which was introduced from Africa. The giant alien can reach a height of 10ft/3m and causes severe burns when its juices come in contact with the skin.

It is worth noting that hedgerows act as overgrown wildlife corridors, and as a result their existence is becoming more and more desirable as the wild habitats of nature vanish at an unprecedented rate because of new farming methods.

(17) The road arrives at a rear entrance to Ashford Castle and is flanked on the left by a delightful lodge. Pass through the limestone pillars and continue STRAIGHT on until you come to a T-junction with a grassy island in the middle. Ignore any of the right turns that will lead back into the castle's terraced gardens.

(18) At the T-junction, go to the LEFT, following the track out through another rear entrance and on to a tarred road. The road passes a number of private houses and after 0.5ml/0.8km arrives at a crossroads.

Just beyond the T-junction and on your right are some fine specimens of evergreen HOLM OAK (*Quercus ilex*). These were widely planted by Lord Ardilaun, and were one of his favourite trees.

Beyond the houses, the landscape opens up as you pass through the remains of the original castle farm. Fine stone walls, which are adorned with small fronds of MAIDENHAIR SPLEENWORT (*Aspleniun trichomanes*) lead the way, while here and there the odd parkland tall tree remains.

The pigeon hole is a deep limestone chasm into which innumerable stone steps plunge, leading down to its dark interior.

(19) On arriving at the cross roads, with an industrial site on the right, go STRAIGHT through the cross and proceed along the tarred road for 0.25ml/0.4km until you come to a lay-by on the right.

Along the way the old walls are delightfully overgrown with BLACKBERRY (*Rubus*) bushes. Through the tangle of briars the purple-flowered FUMITORY (*Fumaria officinalis*) and yellow MEADOW VETCHLING (*Lathyrus pratensis*) straggle upwards to display their flowers throughout the summer. Both are vigorous climbing plants that use the briars for support as they cannot stand on their own.

(20) At the lay-by surrounded by conifer trees, take the signposted path on your RIGHT into Pigeon Hole Wood. The path leads down through the trees onto a track. Follow the track to the LEFT and after about a hundred metres you arrive at the pigeon hole.

(21) Having reached and visited the pigeon hole, continue STRAIGHT on and follow the delightful footpath through the woods.

The pigeon hole is a deep cavern with a series of steep steps and an iron handrail leading down to the bottom. It is very dark and muddy but after rain you can hear, if not see, another subterranean river as it courses its way down to its exit point at Cong. A pair of enchanted white fish are said to dwell in the river – the ghost-like forms of a loving couple who vanished mysteriously in the area!

(22) Follow the woodland path until you arrive at a tunnel which has an iron gate and arched entrance.

The path wanders through a delightful mix of HAZEL, ASH, MOUNTAIN ASH, BEECH and OAK that rupture through the soft limestone rock. The ground flora of the wood is rich with lots of COMMON DOG VIOLET (*Viola riviniana*), WILD STRAWBERRY (*Fragaria vesca*), WOOD-SORREL, (*Oxalis acetosella*), PRIMROSE (*Primula vulgaris*) and BLUEBELL (*Scilla non-scripta*). These are all spring-flowering species as they have to grow and reproduce before the appearance of the thick tree canopy which blocks out all the light. Keep an eye out for the rare BURNET ROSE (*Rosa pimpinellifolia*) along the path's edge, a plant that thrives on the alkaline limestone. Overhead BLUE TITS (*Parus caeruleus*) and CHAFFINCHES (*Fringilla coelebs*), though hard to spot, can be heard chattering amidst the tangle of branches.

(23) The path arrives at the tunnel which leads under the road and back into Cong wood. Go STRAIGHT through, out the other side and follow the riverside path until you arrive back at point (3). Some woodland clearance has occurred in this vicinity but with a bit of care you should be able to trace the riverside path.

Having come through the tunnel, you will notice the surrounding low cliffs of limestone rocks. It is near the base of these cliffs that the waters of Lough Mask start to emerge and thus give rise to the Cong river. The path stays quite close to the riverbank and should afford some opportunities to see some of the riverside wildlife before arriving at the end of the walk.

(3) On reaching the signposted entrance to Cong Wood, go to the LEFT, back over the footbridge, through Cong Abbey and so to the start of the walk.

11 – Lough Nadirkmore

OVER THE TOWERING PEAKS OF THE PARTRY MOUNTAINS and through the labyrinth of its glaciated coombes and tarns, the unbridled winds blow to toss and buffet a thousand blooms and cast their aromatic scents into the air. On the mountain summits a wild wind whips across the knife-edged crests, wrapping its stinging tentacles about you. The wild hawk kites across the cloud-filled skies and the lone raven echoes from the higher hills as it careers about the cliff-edged corries. Rainbows arc from hill to hill on wet sunny days as the gurgling of youthful streams calls across the heath. Out of dark coombes, mirror lakes reflect jagged cliffs and crumbling precipices that plunge into the bottomless depths. All about is an overwhelming sense of isolation that at first discourages but then seems to offer a freedom and wildness that is unbound.

Here, the empty hills give room for thoughts of peace and a world at one with the universe. Human trauma and conflict seem to belong to another time, while you are liberated to the limitless expanse of mountain wilderness, there to wander as if the last human on earth.

WALK DESCRIPTION

LOCATION: The walk begins near the mouth of the Owenbrin river valley in the Partry mountains and on the western shore of Lough Mask. Travel from Clonbur village along the lakeside road of Lough Mask and on towards Lough Nafooey. After travelling for 8ml/12.8km, watch for a signposted RIGHT turn (R300) for Cois an Bharraigh/Castlebar 44km. Tuar Mhic Eadaigh/Tourmakeady 16km'. Take this RIGHT turn, proceed for 2ml/3.2km and take the next LEFT turn off with signs for IDOMAN TEORANTA and Coill an tSiain. Also adjacent to this junction is the original parish school with a plaque on its front wall 'Scoil Naisiunta An Doire A.D. 1930'. Continue along this side road for exactly 1ml/1.6km to a LEFT turn-off opposite a one-storey cottage surrounded by evergreen trees. At this junction, there is a large open space on the left where you can park. If coming from Leenane, travel south on the R336 for 8km and take the LEFT turn, sign-posted for Lough Nafooey.

TERRAIN: A tough circular walk that climbs up and around the glaciated horseshoe of Lough Nadirkmore (large dark coombe) (625m). It is accessed by means of a rough track but then climbs up the cliffed sides of the coombe and across the featureless terrain atop Maumtrasna Mountain, before descending by means of an equally challenging ridge. The ground underfoot is boggy and wet.

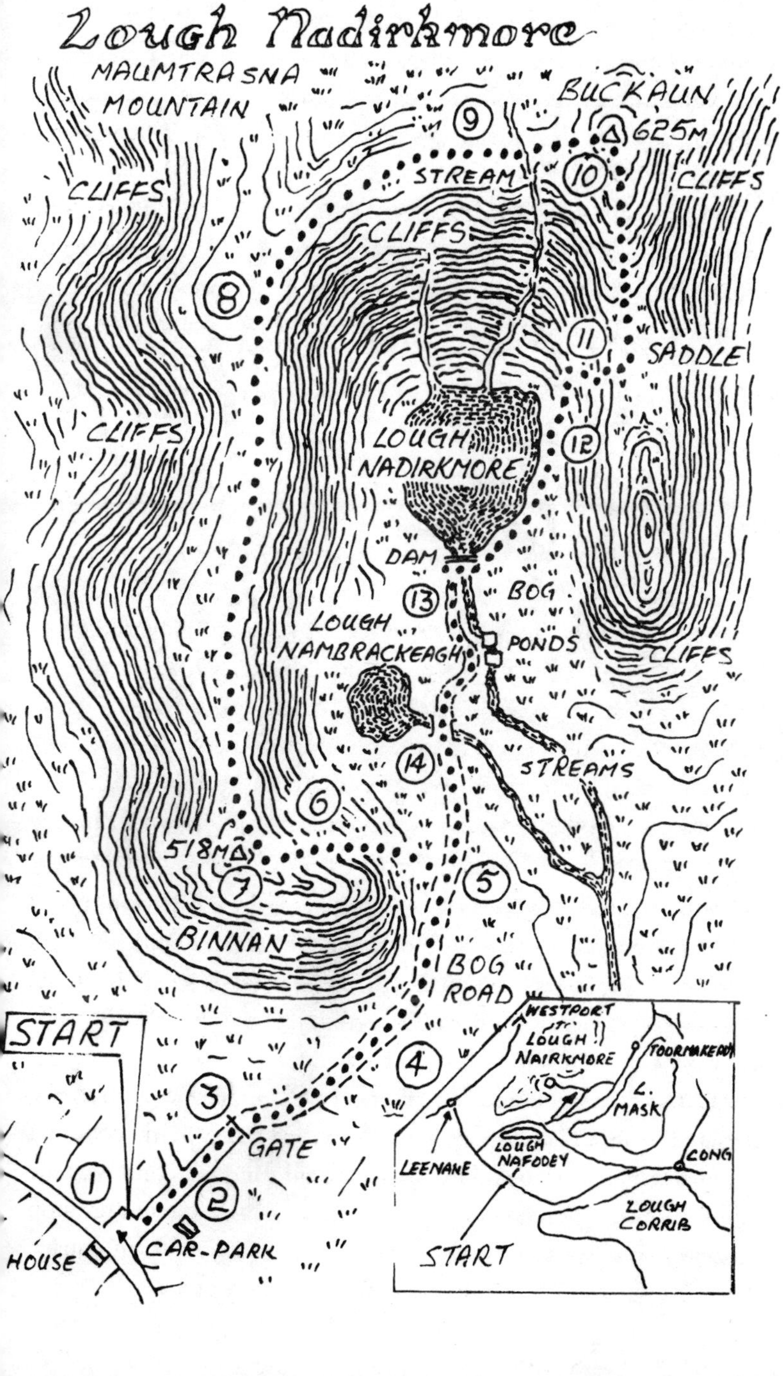

Lough Nadirkmore

MAUMTRASNA
MOUNTAIN

BUCKAUN

⑨

△ 625M

CLIFFS

STREAM

⑩

CLIFFS

CLIFFS

⑧

⑪

SADDLE

CLIFFS

LOUGH
NADIRKMORE

⑫

DAM

BOG
PONDS

⑬

LOUGH
NAMBRACKEAGH

⑭

STREAMS

⑥

518M△

⑦

⑤

BINNAN

BOG
ROAD

START

④

WESTPORT
L. LOUGH
NAIRKMORE

TOORMAKEADY

③

L.
MASK

GATE

①

②

LEENANE

LOUGH
NAFOOEY

CONG

HOUSE

CAR-PARK

START

LOUGH
CORRIB

With their spiky green foliage and bright yellow blossoms, the gorse (left) and the broom (right) may look the same. But their differences may be seen on closer examination.

It is only accessible to those that are fit, agile and have plenty of previous experience with regard to mountain terrain. Additionally, due to its proximity to the western seaboard, the uplands are prone to low cloud, fog and mist. Thus it is not suited to casual walkers. You need to know about weather changes and how to cope with difficult conditions.

FEATURES: Impressive views of the Partry mountains; mountain corrie of Lough Nadirkmore; good views over Lough Mask and the flat plains of east Mayo and Galway; glacial and geological features; upland flora and fauna.

LENGTH: 6ml/10km.

TIME: Needs a minimum of 4 hours, but allow 5.

EQUIPMENT: Waterproof boots with a good grip and ankle support are essential for the upland heath. A knapsack with a supply of food and refreshments. Ordnance Survey Map No. 38. Compass.

WHEN TO WALK: Suitable at any time of the year but best avoided during low cloud and mist when the high ridge of Buckaun becomes dangerous or after torrential rain when the mountain streams are in flood. Obtain a comprehensive weather report before setting out and insure no fog or cloud will occur.

WALK OUTLINE

(1) Having parked at the lay-by follow the tarred road up towards the mountains.

The Partry mountain landscape is hostile to plants, with only a few rare species occurring. Those that do occur, grow with great vigour, for example the common species that are met on the lower foothills. At times, the colours of these wild flowers seem to match each other in each season. Along the way, the old walls are covered with yellow-flowered GORSE (*Ulex europaeus*) and the similarly coloured BROOM (*Cytisus scoparius*), their thickets of golden blossoms heralding the arrival of summer in May and early June. Come the months of August and September, the surrounding dry meadows are awash with COMMON KNAPWEED (*Centaurea nigra*) and RED CLOVER (*Trifolium pratense*), their blood-red flowers signalling the approach of autumn.

(2) Further up by a left turn, the road reverts to a rough track; keep STRAIGHT on.

The dry meadows slowly give way to heath that slopes down towards the valley of the Owenbrin river on your right. Further up the river, large tracts of coniferous plantation cloak the lower mountain sides. These recall ancient times when the valley was blanketed with a dense coniferous forest of SCOTS PINE (*Pinus sylvestris*) about eight thousand years ago. Large areas of their fossilised tree trunks can still be found beneath the cut-away bogs, and some will be encountered up ahead. But many of these are rather small and easily overshadowed by the large and impressive examples found near the mouth of the Owenbrin river and around the neighbouring shores of Lough Mask. Indeed, the treeless landscape of much of present-day Mayo hardly earns its ancient Celtic name, Maigh Eo – 'the plain of the yew trees'.

(3) Soon a gate crosses the track. Open and re-close, maintaining a STRAIGHT course.

As you climb higher, better views of Lough Mask unfold behind you with the flat plain of east Mayo fading into the hazy distance. Straight across the lake is the town of Ballinrobe, an area steeped in history. In the last century, a certain Captain Boycott lived in Lough Mask House, acting as land agent for the absentee landlord, Lord Erne, and collecting extortionate rents from his long-suffering tenants. Pressed beyond endurance, the people of Ballinrobe and the district encouraged the captain's servants to abandon him, and successfully organised his complete isolation. Unable to harvest crops or continue with the operation of the estate, the captain eventually retreated from the district, leaving his name to stand for a new and peaceful tactic in the resistance of oppression.

Looking more closely at Lough Mask, you may note that it has no visible exiting rivers. This is due to the fact that the lough is surrounded by a layer of porous limestone through which the water flows into Lough Corrib via a system of underground rivers. Even more curious is the fact that the level of the lough water appears to have actually fallen by as much as 15ft/4.5m since the last century. The famous Irish botanist, Robert Lloyd Praeger, attributed some of this drop to the 'construction of the futile Mask-Corrib canal, through the floor of which the water pours as through a sieve' (*see* Cong walk).

(4) The track follows the contour of the mountain as it climbs up and around the heather-clad slope on the left.

All around, the shadowed and steep walls of the eroded mountains loom large. Overhead the raucous honking of HOODED CROWS (*Corvus corone cornix*) and RAVENS (*Corvus corax*) can be heard regularly echoing about the higher peaks, their lonesome notes adding to rather than taking from the heavenly silence.

The Partry mountains are quite ancient, being composed of Silurian slates and Carboniferous sandstone that were laid down more than four hundred million years ago. The resulting soil is acidic in nature and this is reflected in the impoverished peatland-type flora such as the dominant heathers like LING (*Calluna vulgaris*), BELL HEATHER (*Erica cinerea*) and ST DABEOC'S HEATH (*Daboecia cantabrica*) – a very different growth from the abundance of plants found about the alkaline limestone shores of Lough Mask. There the meadows are full of colourful blossoms that include such notables as the CARLINE THISTLE (*Carlina vulgaris*) and the YELLOW-WORT (*Blackstonia perfoliata*). In fact, this change in vegetation is so marked that where the acidic sandstone meets the alkaline limestone as, for example, west of the village of Partry near the northern end of the lough, there is a noticeable difference in the flora almost from one side of the road to the other.

(5) As the track begins to level out near the top the inner recess of the coombe opens up before you. On the left is the ridge of Binnaw while further in to the right is the ridge of Buckaun. Both form the characteristic arms of this wonderful coombe.

Leave the track here by going to the LEFT and climb up the back or north facing side of Binnaw. This is best done by locating the sloping sward of grass between the more rugged and cliffed slopes. Following this up, it makes an easily traversible climb to the top.

Carved out by the cutting edge of mile-high glaciers, the valley of the Owenbrin river incises deeply into the very heart of this mountain mass. During the last great Ice Age, which covered vast stretches of west Mayo, much of the ice sheet was centred about the high point of Maumtrasna (2207ft/670m), the peak hidden behind the high cliffs in front of you. As a result, the greatest influence of the glaciers was in this region, forming the valley of the Owenbrin and the many spectacular glacial tarns that are encountered about these hills. None is more impressive than the beautiful Lough Nadirkmore that as yet is hidden from view but will presently be seen.

(6) As you rise, better and better views into the inner recess of the glaciated coombe unfold. The smaller Lough Nambrackeagh appearing first, and as you rise higher the large expanse of Lough Nadirkmore becomes visible. This lake beautifully illustrates the spectacular sculpturing effect of the ice as it retreated from the mountain tops.

In summer the wet, heathery slopes are awash with yellow TORMENTIL blue-flowered HEATH MILKWORT and the red-tentacled leaves of the insect-eating SUNDEW.

Overhead, RAVENS regularly glide on the rising winds, their kronking calls echoing hypnotically about this natural amphitheatre and binding one's soul to the wild uplands. Confined primarily to the west-coasts of Ireland and England, it is sad to know that there may now be only 5000 pairs left. Their loss from the wilderness would greatly impoverish its character. Individuals and state bodies should therefore take all necessary measures to ensure that sufficient of these wild habitats are left intact and do not fall victim to intensive farming or forestry.

About the shoreline of the small lough is a variety of aquatic plants, some forming expansive carpets across the water's surface. Mountain tarns are usually very deep, cold and lacking in nutrients, so it is quite unusual to see such a rich luxuriance of plant life. This richness will become more marked when you compare it to Lough Nadirkmore later on. You may manage to spot the straw-like stands of the unusual, and exceedingly rare, North American-based PIPEWORT (*Eriocaulon aquaticum*) growing amidst the relatively common stands of similarly-shaped HORSETAIL (*Equisetum*). The large floating carpets around the opposite side of the tarn are the lance-shaped leaves of PONDWEED (*Potamogeton*).

(7) On reaching the top at 518m, follow the ridge as it swings to the RIGHT, maintaining a west-northwest direction, and work your way around the horseshoe. Consisting of an open plain of stones, rock and peat hags, there is no prominent peak here, nor any further substantial rise in height. Thus the walking from here on is relatively easy. The delights of this place are to be found in the magnificent views now visible.

Watch out for the four-spotted libula dragonfly which can be seen perching on the lakeside 'horsetails'.

Looking back east there are fine views out over Lough Mask and to the flat plains of County Mayo beyond. Further south is the adjacent Lough Corrib that runs down to Galway city. From up here it is easy to see how both lakes formed a natural defensive barrier in ancient times, separating the tribal lands of the mountainous west from the central plain.

(8) Approaching the back of the coombe, begin turning to the RIGHT, first heading north and later turning north-east. However, maintain a respectable distance from the cliffed sides.

The stunning amphitheatre of towering cliffs and spliced rock that surrounds this glacial tarn is most inspiring. From a height of almost 1000ft/300m, two tinselled waterfalls spill down upon the lower slopes of piled scree at the rear end of the lough. After heavy rain, the coombe echoes to their swollen cascades as they roar across the dark-grey waters in a white foaming, thunderous clamour.

(9) A small stream will eventually be crossed (when it is not raining), after which you ascend up to the higher ground in front of you, to the top of Buckaun at 625m. This is marked by a small pile of stones.

Stretching back from the coombe, the whole top of Maumtrasna is an expansive, featureless plain of thin boggy heath. However, it is surrounded on most sides by treacherous cliffs, thus it is not the place to get lost in fog.

(10) Arriving at the top of Buckaun (625m) brings one to the

The many varieties of bumblebee can be difficult to distinguish, but some features do tell them apart. *Left*: common carder bee – all-over orange colour. *Centre*: garden bumblebee – yellow stripes and white tail. *Right*: large red-tailed bee – black, with bright orange tail.

northern side of the coombe and the descending arm of the horseshoe. Turn to the RIGHT and work your way carefully down through the rocky outcrops onto the saddle of Buckaun. This is a rather steep incline, and should not be rushed.

While you are taking a rest to absorb some further views from Buckaun, a short trek to the north brings one to another cliffed precipice. This plunges down into the equally-formed Dirkbeg Lough. Beyond the lake and over the distant hills the holy mountain of Croagh Patrick is visible on a clear day.

(11) Having arrived onto the saddle, maintain a STRAIGHT course for a few metres, then begin to work your way, slowly and carefully, down the steep slope on the RIGHT and make for the shoreline of the lough. The descent is best done in a zig-zag fashion, following the grassy, stepped ledges until the bottom is reached. DO NOT walk out to the front of this ridge as it is not possible to descend from its cliffed front.

(12) Having reached the lough shore, go to the LEFT and cross the exit stream by means of the concrete weir. Avoid the expanse of water-logged bog between the ridge and the lough.

Crossing the boggy heath, beware of the very soft and waterlogged ground on your right. Around the low vegetation, COMMON BLUE DRAGONFLIES (*Enallagma cyathigerum*) and FOUR-SPOTTED LIBULA DRAGONFLIES (*Libellula quadrimaculata*) may be met during the summer months. These delightful insects spend the winter months as larval forms in the muddy bottoms of pools and vegetation-choked boggy callows. Sheets of stunted heather pour down the weathered valley slopes and stream-carved gullies. The murmur of falling water drifts away into the shadows of these age-old mountains which seem to be quietly meditating as life and time itself pass.

(13) Beyond the weir a rough lane leads you down past some deep tanks of water which are part of the local water supply scheme. Avoid the tanks and continue to follow the track until the original bog road is reached.

This area held a greater concentration of people in the mid-nineteenth century, with numerous small villages in the sheltered valleys. Then, much of the land around here and in the neighbouring townland of Tourmakeady was under the control of the protestant Archbishop of Tuam, Dr Plunkett, who discriminated against his Catholic tenants and regularly evicted them in all sorts of weather. Looking at an angle to your left, you may notice a rough track clinging to the valley sides. Beyond this track and over the ridge is the valley of Glensaul. On a cold November night in 1859, the Archbishop's dreaded crowbar brigade, backed up by a large party of bailiffs and police, arrived at Glensaul to evict sixty of the tenants. All the houses were demolished and the families, including young, sick and old, were thrown out on the roadside to die of hunger and exposure. Such acts greatly depopulated the region and produced their own inevitable backlash. The region was the stomping ground of Father Lavelle, who like many others fought tirelessly against landlord oppression.

(14) Once back on the bog road maintain a STRAIGHT course, following it back down to the start of the walk.

Much of the lane's hedgerows are covered in the delightful red-flowered FUCHSIA (*Fuchsia magellanica*) bushes through which thread strongly-scented ROSES, their sweet aroma hanging heavily on a summer evening's air. Where the hedgerow is more overgrown, the odd PEACOCK BUTTERFLY (*Inachis io*) and SMALL WHITE BUTTERFLY (*Pieris rapae*) hovers about the nectar-rich blossoms. The fuchsia blossoms will be a-hum with nectar-seeking BUMBLEBEES. Any large bumblebees you see in the spring are probably queen bees that have emerged from hibernation and are now getting ready for the breeding season when they must retire to the hive and produce a new colony. Those bees that you see in early to mid-summer are the sterile female worker bees, tirelessly collecting pollen and nectar for the growing brood. Lastly, those you see in the late summer are probably the stingless male bees that have been ejected from the hive, their job of fertilisation done.

12 – Tonakeera Point

WALKING THE MILES OF wave-lashed shoreline has a special flavour all of its own. Mighty rollers pour in from the sea in thunderous applause at your passing and the salty winds fill your lungs with a freshness that enlivens your spirit.

The west coast of Ireland bears the brunt of much of the Atlantic Ocean's temper when wild storms break against its rugged coastline. Many a life has been lost to the sudden eruption of frothing seas that whip the exposed coastline in a stinging gale. Rock and island are stripped of all but the hardiest of life forms while mountainous cliffs crumble before the unrelenting assault.

But when the storm has abated the sea lies calm and tranquil, the energies of its spent force covered over with a charisma and romance that draw one-and-all to marvel at its beauty. Clean golden sands fade away to distant horizons of green-mantled dunes, radiant blue skies stretch cotton clouds into streaks of feathered white, while the hypnotic rise, break and fall of the lace-fringed waves work deeply into one's consciousness.

South of Clew Bay on the south-western extremity of county Mayo, great stretches of golden beach run for miles along the Atlantic front, while gently curved dunes run back from the broad strands to wrap around the feet of the heather-clad hills. Cut off from the outside world by the encircling raw steep sides of the Mweelrea mountains, Tonakeera Point possesses a wildness that is beautifully devoid of human intrusion, exuding a spirit of unspoilt freedom.

WALK DESCRIPTION

LOCATION: The walk starts at the beach of Silver Strand, south east of Tonakeera Point, situated 10ml/16km from Louisburgh. Approaching Louisburgh from Westport, go STRAIGHT through the village and maintain a STRAIGHT course with the road signposted for Silver Strand/Kileen/Roonagh pier R378 (do not turn off for Roonagh pier). After 5ml/8km, pass STRAIGHT through the village of Kileen (just a church and a school on opposite sides of the road). Follow the road to its very end, but be careful as the last few miles are very narrow and care must be taken during the busy summer season.

TERRAIN: This is extensive sheep farming country, thus NO DOGS please. A delightful casual and longitudinal walk across low coastal heath and along an expansive stretch of golden beach. Suitable for both the casual stroller and the more experienced walker who likes a relaxing day's walk when the high mountains are shrouded in cloud and inaccessible.

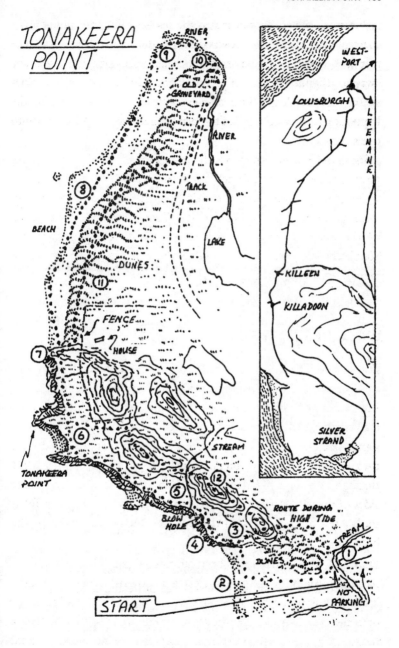

FEATURES: Miles of golden beach; seashore wildlife; dunes with associated flora and fauna; fabulous sea views to the offshore island of Inishturk and Clare Island; coastal mountain scenery.

LENGTH: 5ml/8km.

TIME: 3.5–4 hours.

EQUIPMENT: Comfortable walking boots or wellingtons. Windproof jacket as the area is quite exposed to the wind and you can become quite cool if you stop to rest.

WHEN TO WALK: Suitable at any time of the year when the weather is dry and warm. However, large tracts of the beach are covered at high tide and you then have to stick closer to the upper shoreline by the dunes. During the high spring tides, as the water floods the road and heath, you may not be able to access the dunes. You will then have to be patient and wait for the tide to ebb.

Walking in such remote areas is not recommended during stormy weather for obvious reasons. And during rare hot summer Sundays, the beach at the walk's start can be quite busy and the small road leading to it becomes irritatingly congested.

WALK OUTLINE

(1) A small stream separates the beach from the road. Cross this by using the timber footbridge provided and then walk STRAIGHT down towards the seashore.

Quite a lot of strange objects get washed up on a beach, much to the delight of the beachcomber. The high concentration of beached JELLYFISH in summer is fascinating. You can also discover objects of a very different nature. The North Atlantic Drift that sweeps across from the Gulf of Mexico and up the west coast of Ireland can bring with it quite large seeds from as far as Jamaica. These are extremely hard and bean-shaped and in former times were collected by young girls as love charms to put under their pillow at night.

(2) On reaching the water's edge, turn to the RIGHT and work your way up on to the coastal heath, following the high watermark. This is considerably easier to do at low tide; when the tide is in you will have to climb up through the dunes.

The shore crab is one of the most common species found on our shoreline and is a frequent occupant of rock pools.

Sea sand, because of its shifting and unstable nature, is not normally conducive to animal life, little if any being found in the deep drifts of dry sand. But where the tide reaches, a number of creatures have learned to exploit the potential that is available. Burrowing deep into the sand when the tide is out, the many marine bristle worms and bivalve molluscs evade detection, springing into action again when the tide returns. Thus the lower shoreline will contain the greatest quantity of marine fauna. Here the presence of BRISTLE WORMS (*Polychaeta*) is indicated by the coiled worm casts they throw up on top of the sand.

Controlled primarily by the pull of the moon and to a lesser extent by the sun, the tides fall and rise twice daily. The daily lunar cycle is twenty-four hours and fifty minutes, so the tides are fifty minutes later each day. Every two weeks, during the new and full moon, when the moon and sun lie closely in line, there are wider-ranging spring tides. During the first and last quarter moon, there are lower-ranging neap tides. Spring tides are higher and recede further, while neap tides show very little variation between the high and low watermark. Thus the best time to see the sand-dwelling fauna is during the spring tides when the greatest expanse of the lower shore is exposed. Additionally, during the spring (21 March) and autumn (21 September) equinoxes the most spectacular spring tides occur. Then the moon and the sun are directly in line and the tide recedes to an incredible distance, exposing a part of the lower shore that is not normally seen. For a short few days you get a privileged glimpse of the rich bounty of burrowing creatures that survives deep in the sand.

(3) When up on the heath, go to the LEFT, walking above the rocks and out to the promontory's end.

The short sward of grassy heath has a variety of common plants growing on it such as EYEBRIGHT (*Euphrasia*), HAWKWEED (*Hieracium*) and BOG PIMPERNEL (*Anagallis tenella*). Amongst the flowers lie numerous limpet shells, the scavenged remains of what the predatory gulls have managed to prise from the rocks.

When the tide is out, the various rockpools exposed around the lower shoreline contain the most fascinating and diverse collection of marine life forms. To observe rockpools at their best, crouch discreetly by the water's edge and wait for the various residents to display themselves. Around the edges, a variety of seaweeds and crannied rocks conceal the various inhabitants. Jelly-like and jewel-coloured ANEMONES (*Actinia equina*) stick securely to the pool sides, their feeding tentacles ready to grab at any passing prey. TOPSHELLS (*Calliostoma*) graze the algae-covered rocks, leaving a distinctive feeding trail behind them, CRABS scurry about the bottom, small SHRIMP, GOBY and BLENNY FISH dart from one crevice to the next, and a varied collection of hard coraline algae adds an iridescence to the rocky bottom. The list is endless, with no two rockpools exactly alike. You may even encounter groups of the curious SLIPPER LIMPET (*Crepidula fornicata*), which changes its sex from male to female as it reaches full growth. Perhaps this is only to be expected with a Latin name like that!

(4) On nearing the end of the promontory, turn to the RIGHT and continue to follow the outline of the rocky coastline. Take care when near the wave-washed rocks and be careful of the small blowhole found near the edge of the heath ahead.

Here you may notice the large variety of objects washed up on the rocks. After a strong gale the occasional dead whale is encountered, an indication of the presence of these mammals in our coastal waters. Unfortunately, many are injured by boats or choked by discarded

Watch out for the ever-present oystercatchers along the shoreline.
You will recognise them by their black and white colouring

plastic debris. But it is also heartening to know that Ireland is now an internationally recognised whale and dolphin sanctuary, the second largest in the world. In order to facilitate a greater knowledge of the state of these animals any finds should be reported to the zoology department of the nearest university.

(5) Further on, a small stream must be crossed. Beyond this you may spot a number of parallel ridges in the heath, running at right angles to the shoreline. These are the remains of very old potato lazy beds which would have been tilled by the large local population. They are some of the vast amount of such plots scattered through this wild mountainous territory – a legacy from a dark past when the beleaguered people of the nineteenth century were forced to live in the most inhospitable wildernesses.

(6) Some distance ahead, you arrive at a fine pocket beach enclosed by a rim of low rocky outcrops. If the tide is out, the beautiful strip of virginal sand lures one down. Then the varied forms of seaweed that cover the rocks can be observed. These marine algae are reminiscent of the first plants to attempt a colonisation of the land many millions of years ago, well before any form of animal crawled upon it. They have no true roots, stems or leaves, other than a clinging holdfast that does not draw sustenance from, but merely grips, the barren rock, and a stipe that attaches but does not transport nutrients to the strap-like fronds. Nor can it stand up when the tide is out; instead it lies flat on itself, smothering the lower layers and stopping all photosynthetic activity. Thus it never succeeded in colonising dry land and remained imprisoned in the sea.

On the rocks, look for the grape-like bunches of BLADDER WRACK (*Fucus vesiculosus*) which has paired air bladders along its fronds and SPIRAL WRACK (*Fucus spiralis*) which never has air bladders. Less conspicuous but still present are the smaller clumps of edible CARAGEEN MOSS (*Chondrus crispus*) which has brown-red to green fern-like fronds. You may find the long whip-like stipes of OAR-WEED (*Laminaria digitala*) washed up on the strand; this algae grows attached to rocks of the lower shore and in the sea to depths of 100ft/30m.

On the rocks, OYSTERCATCHERS (*Haematopus ostralegus*) are regularly seen and are easily recognised by their black-and-white colouring and conspicuous long red beak. These feed on the various shelled bivalves that are exposed at low tide, and so they tend to stay near the shore. Another common bird of the coastline is the white diving GANNET (*Sula bassana*). Wary of humans, these summer visitors stick to offshore rocks where they breed in large colonies. Clare Island, visible up along the coast, has the fourth largest colony in Ireland. They are quite noticeable as they dive arrow-like into the sea after the shoals of fish they can see under the water. You may also encounter the resident RINGED PLOVER (*Charadrius hiaticula*) that runs about the beach and, in winter, the quick-dashing SANDERLING

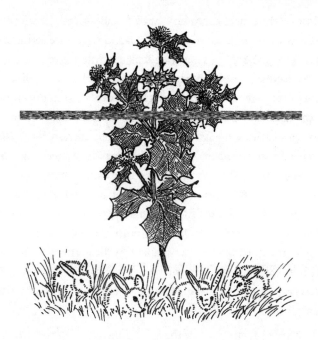

Numerous rabbits will be found around the dunes, but the purple-flowered sea holly is a formidable match for these voracious nibblers, its spiky leathery leaves offering ample self-protection.

(*Calidris alba*) can be spotted as it runs to and fro in front of the breaking waves.

(7) Further ahead, you pass through a gap in a low stone wall and then climb up on to a rocky buttress that drops to the sea in a series of low cliffs.

From the top of the rock the views ahead along the beach are quite unexpectedly breathtaking. Stretching up along the coast for almost two miles, the golden sands contrast vividly with the bright blue, white-crested sea. The multitude of rocky islets offshore and the outlines of Inishbofin (island of the white cow) and Inishturk (island of the boar) are easily seen on your left, providing a mystical backdrop to this enchanting beach. You could probably walk from here for 8ml/13km along the coast to Clew Bay and remain on a beach for almost all of the journey, but private property rights might prevent this.

(8) Once on the beach, continue to walk for about 1ml/1.6km until the long stretch of sand dunes comes to an end and a river crosses the strand.

On a fine blue-skied day, as one walks by the retreating tide and rushing flotsam, one's thoughts wander with the spell-binding rhythm of the waves. The reason for the sea's almost hypnotic power over the human spirit must surely lie buried deep within the subconscious, drawing its strength from our distant past. At that stage, that which would evolve into *Homo sapiens* existed as an aquatic organism in the sea. This in time developed from fish into amphibian (like the frog), and later into fur-skinned mammals, some of which evolved into the primates that ultimately produced us. Nonsense, you may say, but then why does the human foetus have gills on its neck up to the third week of pregnancy? As the foetus matures it goes through its own evolutionary process as the gills develop into lungs and lower jaw, until by the seventh week the foetus is distinctly human.

(9) On coming to the end of the sand dunes turn to the RIGHT and walk up to the end of the dunes.

With luck the tide is out when you visit and you can stay close to the lower shoreline. Then the end of the sand dunes will be a considerable distance away over on the RIGHT.

Off-shore are the islands of Inishbofin on the left, Inishturk in the middle and Clare Island far to the right. It was on Inishbofin that the 'Pirate Queen' Granuaile's old ally, the Spanish or Turkish pirate Bosco, had his castle refuge. From his adventures at sea, he would return to the safety of the island's excellent harbour, where a chain, stretched across its mouth, thwarted would-be assailants.

Inishbofin also represents the last bastion of resistance by the old Gaelic rulers against the invading Cromwellian forces in the seventeenth century. After Cromwell had conquered the mainland of Connemara, the combined forces of the Irish still held out on Inishbofin. However, by 1653, all resistance to English rule had been crushed and Inishbofin was converted into a type of concentration camp for Irish soldiers, teachers, scholars and priests, their lonely prison being a windswept blowhole. Cromwell had a large fortified castle built above the island's safe harbour and it became the strategic centre for his maritime operations in Connemara. Today the ruins of the castle still stand and the prison blowhole is visible on the north-eastern side of the island.

(10) On reaching the end of the dunes it is time to turn back and work your way through the dunes.

On the washed sand, the strings of BOOTLACE (*Chorda filum*) lie curved and weaved like the lettering of some undeciphered oriental language. About the upper tidemark is a clutter of shells and plastic rubbish. When you look at the dunes to the right, keep an eye out for a rough collection of stones. This is the remains of an old graveyard that was used by the large population that lived here in pre-famine times. Most were evicted, but many more died of hunger, leaving the area depopulated to this day. Up in the hills, you can still see the remains of many of the former dwellings of these people, some of whom surely lie buried here.

The dunes are covered with the dominant MARRAM GRASS (*Ammophila arenaria*), a prime agent in the formation of the dune system as its wide rooting system holds the sand together. Little else grows at the front of the dune system but as you move inland to its rear the diversity of coastal species increases. Two of the more characteristic flora are SEA HOLLY with its leathery spiked leaves (*Eryngium maritimum*) and COMMON REST-HARROW (*Ononis repens*).

(11) Passing back along the dunes a house surrounded by fencing is visible on the left. Keep close to the seaward side of the dunes and avoid the fenced area until you arrive back at the original point (7).

The dry sandy heath has a variety of characteristic and common grassland flora. PUFF-BALLS (*Lycoperdon*) are plentiful towards the summer's end, the ripe and rounded spheres bursting open to release their many spores in the autumn. The heath itself turns yellow during favourable summers with the blossoms of BUTTERCUP (*Ranunculus acris*) and HAWKWEED (*Hieracium*).

RABBITS burrow through the sandy embankments, on which can be found the yellow-flowered SEA PANSY (*Viola curtisii*), WILD THYME (*Thymus praecox*) and KIDNEY VETCH (*Anthyllis vulneraria*) in mid-summer. Earlier in the spring there are plenty of the EARLY-PURPLE ORCHIDS (*Orchis mascula*) and the more common DAISY (*Bellis perennis*).

(7) Return by the outward route back to point (6) keeping the stone wall and fencing to your left.

(6) When the stone wall and fence come to an end the heath opens up again on the left. This allows you to climb up on to the higher ground on the LEFT from which you can still work your way back to the start of the walk at point (1).

The terrain undulates over some rocky clefts and through some soggy patches. A number of potato lazy beds and a few stone walls are encountered, but avoid knocking any of these and try to keep the rocky shoreline visible down on your right.

(12) On reaching the last high hill continue on a STRAIGHT course to arrive back at the start. Keep to the landward side of this hill for easy descent and on approaching Silver Strand pass down through the dunes and out on to the beach at the walk's start.

From the top of this last hill there are fabulous views to the Mweelrea mountains in front of you, with the peak of Mweelrea itself forming the highest point in the west. Beneath the mountain, the mouth of Killary Harbour is visible just beyond the golden sands. The entrance to Killary fjord is indicated by the tall pillars atop the small rocky islands. Across the bay is the large rounded ridge of Tully mountain, at the bottom of which is Renvyle Castle, Granuaile's home when she was the dominant force in Connemara in the sixteenth century.

13 - Croagh Patrick

IRELAND HAS HAD A TUMULTUOUS HISTORY that fades back into pre-recorded days, lost in a confusion of myth, half-truth and legend. Surviving the onslaught of invasion after invasion and the many battles of king, queen, serf, druid and martyr, a single thread runs through all human exploits and remains as solidly ingrained in the Celtic heart today as it did five thousand years ago. Underlying the nature of all human existence is the belief in and reverence for a higher order which we all at one time or another must accept or reject. Situations may change but fundamentals always remain the same. Be it the naive Stone-Age man or present-day intellectual, we will forever look to mother earth to provide the focus through which we can both express and acknowledge our beliefs.

The isolated peak of Croagh Patrick sits on the southern shore of Clew Bay with panoramic views over land and sea, a place where that giver of life, the sun, could be worshipped in all its awe-inspiring glory. And so this mountain became, by virtue of its physical aspect and location, Ireland's holiest of mountains and a site of pilgrimage that dates back several thousand years. In ancient days, when a mix of legend and magic answered the human's most basic understanding of life, the desire to acknowledge the presence of an outer force was as compelling as it is today. Thus it was to the peak of Croagh Patrick that the ancient races of Ireland were ultimately drawn to express their inner desires in whatever way was possible. In time, successive waves of migration and invasion wove the pattern of belief to a different colour offering solace and peace to all those that came and followed. The colour of the cloak may have changed but the pattern remains unaltered, and today the pilgrimage to Croagh Patrick retains that great yearning for answers as steadfastly as it did in times past. Possibly only when we discover a peace and harmony within ourselves, with one another and with our own planet, shall we understand the true meaning of life on earth.

WALK DESCRIPTION

LOCATION: The walk begins 2ml/3.2km west of Westport town. From the town's Octagon go STRAIGHT up the steep hill, ignoring the main road that swings off to the right. A little beyond the top of the hill and at a T-junction go to the LEFT over the bridge and then immediately RIGHT, following the signposted road for the Scenic route to Louisburgh. Continue STRAIGHT on for 1.5ml/2.4km to the old graveyard of Aughavale with its LEFT turn-off. Turn up here and park in the car park of the modern cemetery.

TERRAIN: A moderate circular walk that at first follows some of the minor backroads, then climbs on to the moors along an old green road,

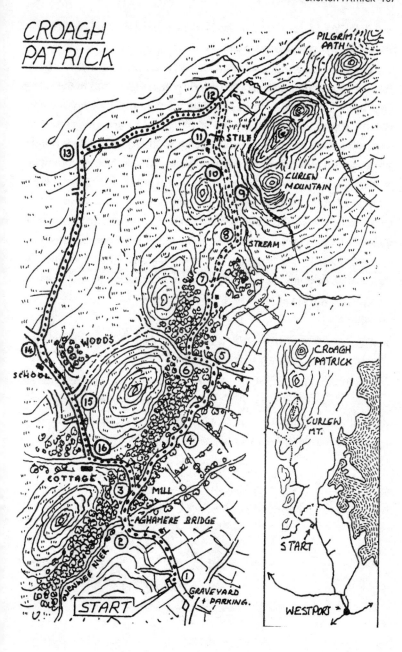

CROAGH PATRICK

PILGRIM PATH

CURLEW MOUNTAIN

STILE

STREAM

WOODS

SCHOOL

COTTAGE

MILL

AGHAMERE BRIDGE

OWENEE NGER

START

GRAVEYARD + PARKING.

CROAGH PATRICK

CURLEW MT.

START

WESTPORT

to finally cross a heather-clad ridge beneath the mountain's peak before returning by the outward route.

NOTE: The well-known route to the top of Croagh Patrick is by an extremely tough but well-marked pilgrim route that begins in the village of Murisk and can be easily followed by any visitor. You do not require a map or text to walk this route but a willingness to share the experience with numerous fellow pilgrims. However, for those who wish to wander more freely about the surrounding hills and dales of the holy mountain, walking the sylvan by-roads and empty moors is just as rewarding. Here, all the beauty and enchantment of the area can be savoured with no less pleasure than if you had climbed the strenuous slopes of the lofty reek.

FEATURES: Wooded country lanes; mountain heath; panoramic views of Croagh Patrick, the surrounding mountainous landscape and the spectacular, drumlin-cluttered Clew Bay; countryside flora and fauna.

LENGTH: 7ml/11km.

TIME: 4 hours.

EQUIPMENT: Comfortable walking shoes, a knapsack to carry refreshments and additional clothing.

WHEN TO WALK: Suitable at any time of the year when there is no rain or mist to spoil the views. Particularly impressive on the sunnier cold days of late autumn or winter when the air is clearer and the high mountain masses sport their snow-capped peaks.

The ruins of an old mill, in their romantic setting on the wooded hillside by the Owenwee river.

WALK OUTLINE

(1) At the other end of the roadside car park, locate the Y-junction and take the RIGHT fork, following the tarred road down towards the river. (You can generally ignore the black poles with the yellow walker symbol.)

The countryside is varied and picturesque with wooded hillsides of SILVER BIRCH (*Betula pendula*) running down to meet the fertile meadows of the Owenwee river valley, its banks choked with a tangled canopy of WILLOW (*Salix*) and ALDER (*Alnus*). Boundary hedgerows hold thickets of HOLLY (*Ilex*), BLACKTHORN (*Prunus spinosa*) and the occasional sentried stand of ASH (*Fraxinus excelsior*) and BEECH (*Fagus sylvatica*), out of whose crowns disturbed WOODPIGEONS (*Columba palumbus*) clatter. Above the woods, rocky knolls are cloaked with thickened sheaves of BRACKEN (*Pteridium aquilinum*) over which the kite-like KESTREL (*Falco tinnunculus*) hovers with winnowing wings in search of small mammals, insects and songbirds. Far away to the right, heather-clad slopes run upwards to the conical top of Croagh Patrick. Its isolated peak looks regal on cloudless days or mysterious and foreboding when shrouded in the swirling mists of thunderous clouds that roll in from the wild Atlantic.

(2) The road drops down to the Owenwee river, across Aghamere bridge and then uphill to a Y-junction.

Approaching the bridge, you see the crumbling remains of an old mill amongst the trees on the hill to the right, its gaunt ivy-clad skeleton a romantic ghost of nineteenth-century industrialisation.

Crossing the bridge, you may spot timber steps descending to the river bank. This is one of the many stiles and paths that follow the river's course upstream, often used by the many fisherfolk in pursuit of the elusive salmon. Spilling over rocky cascades and through swirling pools that are freely accessible from the nearby sea, this short fast-flowing river is richly supplied with tributaries and small loughs, locked within the surrounding mountainous heath. Thus its waters are

You will smell the stinkhorn fungus before you see it. It is usually well hidden in the dank foliage beneath the trees.

suitably clean and oxygen-rich to attract the returning shoals of spawning salmon that appear in Clew Bay each summer. Moving upstream in search of gravel beds, the adult salmon breed in autumn after which they usually die. Their offspring then spend as much as four years in the river before returning to the sea and migrating to the North Atlantic. Here they may remain for several years before returning to breed in the very same river in which they hatched. It is believed that a keen sense of river smell impregnated at birth guides them back to their place of origin.

(3) Shortly a Y-junction is reached, go to the RIGHT.

The narrow road runs in a straight stretch across the side of the hill, overhung with a thick canopy of HAZEL (*Corylus*) and BEECH (*Fagus*). Though quite attractive and stately, with an impressive display of colour in the autumn, the beech is not a native of Ireland. It was planted extensively in the nineteenth century by resident landlords who attempted to redress the balance of the earlier horrendous deforestation of Ireland. Neither are the many wooded hills around here as permanent a feature as they look. It is more than likely that the area was greatly cleared in the recent past, possibly during the economic recession after World War Two. The scarred landscape has slowly healed itself through the ecological laws of succession which at first produce the pioneering silver birch. This in time is replaced by oak which evolves slowly beneath the shaded canopy of the birch trees.

(4) Continue along the road until you come to a T-junction.

The roadside's wooded hedgerows act as important reservoirs for our displaced woodland wildlife. In fact a mature hedgerow is very much a cross-section of a mature woodland, with practically all the attendant plant species. On top there are the mature climax trees of the upper canopy such as OAK and ASH, beneath these there are the under-storey shrubs like HAZEL, HOLLY and HAWTHORN, while finally the woodland ground flora survives upon the stone walls and roadside margins. As you walk in spring, watch for the woodland species of WOOD ANEMONE (*Anemone nemorosa*), WOOD SORREL (*Oxalis acetocella*), PRIMROSE (*Primula vulgaris*) and COMMON DOG VIOLET (*Viola rivinianna*). In summer, look for the HONEYSUCKLE (*Lonicera periclymenum*), DOG ROSE (*Rosa canina*), HART'S-TONGUE (*Phyllitis scolopendrium*) and MALE FERN *(Dryopteris felix-mas)*. Finally, you may encounter a variety of fungi in the autumn, none more arresting then the putrid-smelling STINKHORN (*Phallus impudicus*). The smell from this curious fungus is not unlike rotting flesh and serves to attract flies that help to spread the spores.

(5) On arriving at the T-junction, go uphill to the LEFT, shortly passing a small lane off to the right.

Where the woods open out, thick sheaves of BRACKEN FERN (*Pteridium*) crowd the roadside margins. From within the dense thickets the tiny WREN (*Troglodytes troglodytes*) calls loudly with a distinctive scolding chirp. In spring, the many other songbirds can also be heard as they claim their breeding territories. These they then proclaim to their rivals by pouring out their hearts in early morning and evening song, a sound so moving that it is one of the last things that I would want to hear if I had to snuff it in the morning!

Still, a pleasure of the Irish countryside, such delightful birdsong is now denied to many citizens of continental Europe. There, shooting of these harmless passerines by enthusiasts has practically decimated the breeding populations of many wild birds. With a totally different ethos to their Irish counterparts, some continental hunters are interested only in quantity shot rather than quality. So swans, robins, blackbirds, wrens and so on, are all fair game unless these shooting tourists are supervised. Irish enthusiasts who are members of recognised clubs have a much healthier attitude, shooting only edible species such as duck and pheasant. They also put a lot of effort into breeding some of these species and look upon our songbirds with a reverence. Unfortunately, with the integration of Europe, the threat of an invasion of such vandalistic hunters is exceedingly possible. Anyone annoyed by such a development must be ready to sing out as loudly as the birds and express their revulsion at this short term exploitation of our environmental resources.

(6) Presently a Y-junction is reached and here you go to the RIGHT. Keep an eye out for a signposted green road that branches off to the left about 0.75ml/1.2km ahead.

The delightful woods of silver birch continue to lead uphill. As the altitude increases the varieties of the trees also begins to change slowly. Very noticeable in the autumn are the red-berried ROWAN or MOUNTAIN ASH (*Sorbus aucuparia*), a tree well-suited to the exposed terrain of high boggy heaths. It is usually the last type of deciduous tree to be encountered towards the upper limit of the tree-line.

Where the trees completely overshadow the road, you should be able to spot plenty of ST PATRICK'S CABBAGE (*Saxifraga spatularis*), a notable plant of the west of Ireland – and it is fitting that it grows well on the saint's mountain. Curiously enough though, the emblem of Ireland, the SHAMROCK (*Medicago lupulina* – 'black medick'), which apparently was used by St Patrick to explain the meaning of the three gods in one, does not grow on Croagh Patrick.

(7) Near the top of the hill and just beyond the houses on the right, there is a green road branching off the road on your LEFT. This will be recognised by a black pole with its walking man and arrow symbol. Leave

the road here, opening and reclosing the metal gate after you and follow the old green road up through the treeless heath.

The vegetation has noticeably changed to the more dominant heathers, so too has the associated fauna. SKYLARKS (*Alauda arvensis*) and MEADOW PIPITS (*Anthus pratensis*) are the characteristic songbirds up here, both of which fly up out of the heather and pour out a warbling song that seems to go on indefinitely. They are hard to tell apart but the skylark is larger and has a more conspicuous stripe or supercilium over the eye.

The curlew has a distinctive, down-curved beak, which it uses effectively for probing in the soft mud.

As summer's end approaches, there are plenty of heather blossoms to supply the needs of wasp and bee that move up from their wild hives in the sheltered woods below. Keep an eye out for the rare ST DABEOC'S HEATH (*Daboecia cantabrica*), its exceedingly large bell-shaped flowers noticeable amongst the COMMON LING (*Calluna vulgaris*) and the CROSS-LEAVED HEATH (*Erica tetralix*). Some fine bunches of this are found growing beside the left-hand stream further up.

(8) As you climb, the views around Clew Bay unfold behind you with the fertile fields of the coastal strip running in around Westport town.

At the inner edge of Westport Bay, a thicket of trees marks the demesne of Westport House. Now the business home of the tenth Marquess of

Sligo, the building has a long history dating back to the Middle Ages. In 1730 John Browne, who later became the First Earl of Altamont, built part of the present house, possibly incorporating sections of a medieval castle that belonged to his O'Malley forebears. In 1778, the Second Earl married the heiress of extensive Jamaican sugar plantations, coming into a fortune which made them the richest family in Ireland during the eighteenth century. As a consequence, they were able to beautify the estate and lay out the town of Westport in its present fashion. The Third Earl became the First Marquess of Sligo and he, along with his descendants, continued to develop the house in the grand manner.

The maintenance of such properties as private homes is no longer realistic and unfortunately, due to crippling rates, the Tenth Earl had contemplated selling or demolishing the house. Thankfully, his son and daughter-in-law, the Earl and Countess of Altamont, decided to develop the house as a tourist attraction in order to defray the enormous maintenance expenses. To date this has proved a successful venture and has made Westport an important tourist destination. As a consequence, one of the main treasure houses of Ireland has been retained intact for future generations, and the present generation of the locality has received a welcome economic boost.

(9) On reaching the top of the hill, the peaks of distant mountains start to become visible. This is the highest point of the walk thus a short rest and a good look back is rewarding.

Looking down on the island-studded bay, you get a perfect view of these innumerable small mounds. The islands are in fact a drumlin swarm that was drowned by the rise in sea level which occurred after the last Ice Age melt-down. When the glaciers filling the bay began to retreat, they dropped their load of debris, to form those characteristic domed hills. With time many have been washed away by the sea, with those that remain having their western sides eroded into vertical cliffs while their landward side retains the original sloping aspect.

Clew Bay is the home of the old Gaelic O'Malley clan, who had their stronghold on nearby Clare Island at the mouth of the bay. It was here in the early sixteenth century that Granuaile, or Grace O'Malley, developed her love of the sea with these islands as playground and a source of livelihood. On the drumlins they kept their great herds of cattle; the waters teemed with fish and the neighbouring mainland was covered in vast oak forests that bristled with wildlife.

Sadly, the English conquerors destroyed all Granuaile possessed and she spent the last days of her life destitute in her Clare Island castle. There, it is said, she slept at night with her last few ships tied to the end of her bed by means of a rope pulled through her bedroom window.

(10) The track now goes downhill again. Keep following it until you reach a tarred road. Just beyond the hill top ignore the stepped stile on the right that leads onto the heath.

Great views of the distant mountains unfold before you. Starting from the left and to the east are the Partry Mountains, behind the waters of Moher Lough. The more rugged cliffs of these hills to the south-east are the back of Walk No 12, Lough Nadirkmore. These run across in front of you to merge with the more rugged peaks of the Sheeffry Hills. The most distant high peak to the extreme right of the range and poking up from behind the Sheeffry's is Mweelrea Mountain. This is the highest mountain in the west, at the back of which lie Walks No 10, Killary Harbour and No. 13, Tonakeera Point.

(11) As the track levels out a number of old stone ruins are passed on the left. There is a wire fence across the track here, but use the gate on the right to pass through, remembering to refasten it after you.

Looking up to the RIGHT the high ridge of Curlew Mountain is quite visible as it runs off to meet the conical peak of the holy mountain, Croagh Patrick.

Curlew Mountain has rich swards of heather covering its slopes of open moorland, one of the preferred breeding sites of the CURLEW

(*Numenicus arquata*). Large flocks of them move up here from Clew Bay, where they nest on the ground. These large brown birds with their long legs and distinctive long, down-curved bills are perfectly adapted to probing for food in the soft mud and turf.

Near the top of Curlew Mountain you should be able to see the outline of an old stone wall, running across the hillside. This is the old demesne wall of the former Murisk estate, and has its own tale to tell. The route of this wall is thought to run along the course of the ancient Tóchair Phádraig or Patrick's Causeway, an age-old pilgrim roadway that has a most compelling history. The now vanished causeway predates St Patrick and is thought to have been built by the druid kings of Connaught as a route from Ballintubber to Croagh Patrick when the mountain was sacred to pre-Christian civilisation for sun worship.

Then the mountain was known as Cruchan Aigle, Aigle being the son of Derg of the Tuatha Dé Danann. One of the Tuatha Dé Danann's mortal gods was Lugh who in the year 3300 BC initiated the harvest festival or the Festival of Lughnasa. It is from Lugh that the month of August gets its Gaelic name, Lughnasa. Interestingly, the present and principal Christian pilgrimage day to Croagh Patrick is on the last Sunday before 1 August, known as Domhnach Chrom Dubh or Garland Sunday. It was to this ancient sacred mountain that St Patrick, the patron saint of all Ireland, is reputed to have come to convert the pagan Celts to Christianity in the year AD 441, successfully destroying much that was evil but retaining what was good of the old pagan ways. He knew that if he was to succeed in converting the pagan multitude to the new Christian beliefs, he would first have to destroy the thousand-year-old belief in the pagan gods and their hold over the people. To eradicate the timeworn ways and their associated sacred sites would have been impossible, instead he merely changed the names of the gods and performed the new Christian rituals at the traditional holy sites. And so he must have begun a wide-ranging conversion of innumerable holy places across the length and breadth of the country.

Former Christian devotees made the 20ml/32km trek from Ballintubber abbey to Croagh Patrick on this day. There are numerous accounts, right up to the nineteenth century, of thousands of pilgrims following the Roman-style causeway to the sacred mountain-top. One such story tells how St Patrick, when leading a pilgrimage along the route, arrived at Liscarney to discover that he had left his missal behind him in Aghagower village. Word was passed down along the line of followers which stretched back almost 3ml/5km to Aghagower. From there, the missal was passed forward from person to person until it reached the saint! Many resting sites, holy wells, mass rocks and medieval ruins line the route with a wealth of fascinating stories that would make a book in themselves. (There has been a recent and successful endeavour to retrace the Tóchair Phádraig. This is outlined in the delightful publication of the same name and forms an enchanting one-way walking route.)

(12) On reaching the tarred road, follow it downhill to the LEFT.

Looking back at Croagh Patrick you will see fine views of its majestic peak. All of 2510ft/760m in height, the mountain-top is covered in quartzite, a slow-weathering rock that disintegrated to form the conical peak known locally as The Reek. Cut deeply into its steep ascent is the well-trodden line of the present pilgrim route, coming up from the village of Murisk on the shore of Clew Bay and leading to a small church on top.

Croagh Patrick is the ultimate prize that St Patrick fought in his conversion of Ireland to Christianity, for it was the pinnacle of pagan domination. It is here that he crowned his achievements. Fasting for forty days and forty nights on the mountain-top, as the story goes, he did battle with the pagan gods. Demons came to attack him in the form of horrendous beasts and serpents. All of these he destroyed, and then he bargained with the new god for the salvation of the Irish people who have steadfastly maintained their belief in Christianity up to the present day.

Today, on Garland Sunday, the number of people that arrive in Murisk to complete the penitential pilgrimage to the hazardous summit, some of them barefoot, runs into thousands.

(13) After about 1ml/1.6km you arrive at another T-junction. Go to the LEFT. Before arriving at this junction the landscape is rather open and bleak, but it does have its moments. Heavily grazed by sheep, it still throws out the white sheets of BOG COTTON or COTTON GRASS (*Eriophorum Sp*) during the summer, their white cotton-bud flowers buffeting in the breeze. You should also notice the many parallel trenches cut into more distant peat bogs by the turf cutter. If there is a good warm spell during the summer this area becomes a hive of activity as the many families of the region cut and harvest the turf.

(14) Another mile of tarred road brings you to another T-junction. Go up to the LEFT, passing the small national school of Breac Cluain (1849) soon on your right.

The road presently enters a delightful little glen. Its righthand slopes covered in the sheaves of BRACKEN FERN (*Pteridium Aquilinum*). The lefthand slopes covered in coppiced woodland, mostly of SILVER BIRCH (*Betula pendula*), some HAWTHORN (*Crataegus*) and a few OAK (*Quercus*). This is a natural woodland, the species present and their distribution giving a clue to the wood's history. All wild woodlands in Irealnd tend to ultimately succeed towards oak. However, silver birch is very much a first coloniser of newly emerging woods. Thus it is quite probable that this wood was clear felled of its dominant oak stand sometime in the past. The present rich predominance of birch indicates that the wood is undergoing a healing process. If left undisturbed it will ultimately succeed to its original dominant oak stand, while the silver birch will have been pushed to the woodland margin. This, of course, would take many, many years. In winter the bright purple-red branches and white trunk of the silver birch are readily distinguished from the more tanned crowns of the few oak. In summer the white bleached trunks of the birch are still visible beneath the overall green canopy.

(15) After another mile the road leaves the glen. Ignore the left turn-off and keep going STRAIGHT. After 0.2ml/0.3km you reach a right turn-off, ignore this and keep on STRAIGHT until you come to another T-junction.

(16) After 0.5ml/0.8km you reach a T-junction with a picturesque one-storey cottage in front of you. Go to the LEFT.

(3) Very shortly you come to a Y-junction which you met on the outward journey. This has a new house on the right. Keep to the RIGHT and follow the road down the hill for 0.6ml/0.9km until you reach the car park.

14 – Achill Head

THERE ARE MANY ASPECTS of this countryside that are both stunning in appearance and moving in effect. The wide expanse of the sea never fails to elicit an emotional response, its ever-changing, surging pulse and diffused light bewitching your very soul. Then there are the lofty mountain peaks that when scaled draw out your sense of awe at the tapestried, unfamiliar world spread beneath you. This unknown land runs off to endless horizons and uncharted wildernesses, tempting you to rush into the enchanted maze of lost and half-forgotten valley folds.

But where mountain and sea collide in steep cliffs, their combined splendour can be stupefying in its appeal. Beneath you, the giant battering ram of the ocean throws itself in great heaving, swelling crests against the solid mountain mass, gnawing it into powerful fortress walls. The thunderous booming and crashing of ruptured waves echoes up from the battlefield of a ceaseless war. Fearless sea birds dive through the whipping wind, careering over the fathomless depths and soaring on the rising currents of air, screaming joy, enjoying freedom as they ride the unfettered winds.

WALK DESCRIPTION

LOCATION: The walk starts at the secluded beach of Keem Strand at the very end of Achill Island. Having crossed Achill Sound, travel west along the main road through the villages of Keel and Dooagh until the road reaches its very end at the delightful Keem Bay. Parking is available within the car park above the beach.

TERRAIN: A tough climb up and over the many peaks that make up this most spectacular line of cliffs. Parts of the route are quite wet under foot, especially the initial climb and the final homeward route through Keem Valley. The cliffs are open and exposed, thus they are not suitable for those with a fear of heights and those with young children should keep them in sight at all times. Please read the section of the book on DANGER, with special reference to cliffs on page 10.

NOTE: Due to the spectacular nature of the cliffs, it is also worth returning by the outward route from point (7).

FEATURES: The most spectacular cliff scenery in all of Ireland; some of Europe's highest sea cliffs; panoramic sea views; coastal flora and fauna; ruined settlements.

LENGTH: 4.5mls/7km.

TIME: 4–4.5 hours.

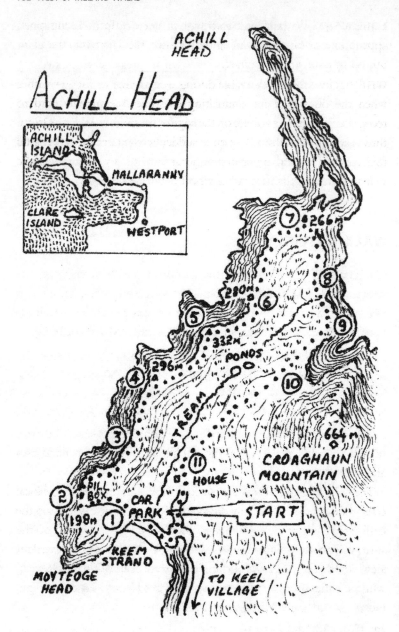

ACHILL
HEAD

ACHILL HEAD

ACHILL
ISLAND

MALLARANNY

CLARE
ISLAND

WESTPORT

⑦ •266

⑧

280m

⑥

⑤

332m

PONDS

296m

④

⑨

⑩

③

STREAM

664m

⑪ □ HOUSE

CROAGHAUN
MOUNTAIN

② PILL
BOX

CAR
PARK

START

① 198m

KEEM
STRAND

MOYTEOGE
HEAD

TO KEEL
VILLAGE

EQUIPMENT: Waterproof boots with a good grip; walking pole; appropriate clothing depending on weather; OS Discovery map No. 30; up-to-date weather report.

WHEN TO WALK: Not suitable during wet, stormy or foggy weather when the outline of the undulating coastline is extremely hard to recognise. Remember you are on the edge of the mighty Atlantic Ocean, thus visibility can become lost quite suddenly when unexpected coastal fogs roll in. This can happen in summer as much as any other time of the year so obtain a reliable weather report before setting out.

WALK OUTLINE

(1) From the car park begin the climb up the steep slope on the western side of the beach. This has a conspicuous earthen fence rising STRAIGHT up. Though very wet under-foot, stay close to this as it leads you up to some conspicuous ruins atop the cliffs of Moyteoge Head.

(2) On reaching the concrete ruins turn to the RIGHT and follow the coastline as it runs northwestwards, towards the first of the many coastal peaks at 296 metres. Be wary of the adjacent cliffs as you walk, keeping a respectable distance from them. There is no official path to follow other than the outline created by previous walkers. Thus you need to stay alert at all times as the cliff line swings in and out and rises and falls unexpectedly.

The concrete ruins were part of a look-out post attached to the local coastguard station, especially during the Second World War. Atop the cliffs at a height of 198 metres they gave a good view of the surrounding ocean that comprises Clew Bay. Today it gives excellent views southeast to Clare Island and the distant cone of Croagh Patrick, while to the south are the many islands off the Mayo coastline, including the larger Inishturk and Inishbofin.

(3) Following the undulating cliff edge, spectacular and dizzy views plummet down to the pounding surf below. Stunted swards of

heather coat the upper ledges, while grassy slopes coat the lower ones. Here, sheep can sometimes be seen grazing, oblivious to the danger. This is when they are at their most vulnerable however, especially to those that are naive enough to bring dogs up here. Then, even the smell of a strange dog, on a lead, can cause them to panic and fall over the cliffs.

(4) There is a steep rise up to the pinnacle at 296 metres, after which the route drops down again before it rises to the highest point of the walk at 332 metres (the Cliffs of Moher weigh in at a pathetic 196m – eat your heart out). Continue to follow the outline of the cliffs with extreme care.

If here during the earlier parts of the summer there is a good chance of seeing the many sea birds that frequent our coastline.

With binoculars you should be able to spot the many RAZORBILLS *(Alca torda)* and PUFFINS *(Fratercula arctica)* that use its safe haven. Both these birds prefer to nest in burrows or under boulders where they cannot be seen.

The sheer cliffs are also extensively occupied by other breeding sea birds. These are hard to spot until they go out to or return from their short fishing forays. Large GUILLEMOT *(Uria aalge)* and SHAG *(Phalacrocorax aristotelis)*, as well as the more gull-like KITTIWAKE

Puffins, comical-looking birds with their parrot-like bills, are rarely seen on our coasts. But they turn up annually in large numbers on the cliffs of Moher each breeding season.

(Rissa tridactyla) and FULMAR *(Fulmarus glacialis)*, can be seen coating the cliffs. Some of these birds do not build a nest but lay their eggs on the cliff ledge. The eggs of the guillemot are pear-shaped so that if they roll, they tend to roll around in a tight circle and not over the edge.

The most common cliff-dwelling bird you will encounter is the fulmar, a superb flier which seems to spend most of the day kiting around the cliff-top on the rising wind draughts. Its wings stiff and dead straight, its short squat tail and characteristic tube-nosed bill make the fulmar readily distinguishable from the common gulls. Some can come quite close to you as they suddenly shoot up from below the cliff. They are birds not to be trifled with while nesting as they vomit the most stinking secretion on top of intruders.

Watch out for the painted lady butterfly flitting about the sea campion on calm sunny days.

(5) On reaching the 332-metre pinnacle, it is worth taking a rest to absorb the stunning views. Behind you is the raw peak of Croaghaun, a great monolith composed of quartzite that plummets in serious cliffs on its seaward that are up to 688 metres high. It is also enriched with Amethyst, a clear purple gemstone, samples of which can be purchased in local craft shops.

(6) Having descended from the 332-metre pinnacle onto a low saddle at 280m, the cliff walk gradually swings to the LEFT as it rises again towards the final high point of 266m. This may seem obvious, but if the fog blows in or low clouds descend this will not be so easy to discern.

As you walk, keep an eye open for the rich coastal flora that adorns these wind swept heights. The famous early twentieth-century Irish botanist Robert Lloyd Praeger visited these cliffs, marvelling at their beauty. Rich swards of purple heather pour down over the cliffs edge, where in fertile pockets the hardy coastal plants thrive.

The pink tufted flowers of THRIFT/SEA PINK (*Armeria maritima*), the open white flowers of SEA CAMPION (*Silene maritima*) and the colourless spikes of SEA PLANTAIN (*Plantago maritima*) are quite common, as they are well able to tolerate the exposed salty conditions. A few rarer cliff-dwelling species, such as the fleshy-leaved ROSEROOT (*Rhodiola rosea*), HEATH PEARLWORT (*Sagina subulata*) and MUSK STORK'S-BILL (*Erodium moschatum*) can also be found. However, these latter plants tend to thrive more on the exposed cliff-face than on the path sides, thus they are harder to find.

Choughs are distinctive crows found along our coasts.
They are easily identified from their bright red beak and legs.

(7) On reaching the final peak of the cliff walk, at 266m the cliff walk ends and one must swing to the RIGHT, dropping down into the low valley that separates you from the dizzy height of Croaghaun mountain to the northeast.

From the apex of the 266m pinnacle, there are wonderful views out over the long spine of 'Little Saddle Head'. It is not advisable to venture out onto this precarious head land, surrounded as it is by unstable cliffs.

Additionally it is more suited to the wild sea birds that need our absence to survive, as in the delightful CHOUGH *(Pyrrhocorax pyrrhocorax)*, those wonderful black, red-beaked and red-legged crows of the coast. Now practically extinct on the European mainland, they are still found in reasonable numbers on the Irish coastline, though declining due to loss of suitable feeding and nesting habitats. As you walk here in summer, their distinctive voice can be regularly heard as the skim about the coastal heath or perch on the rocky pinnacles of this, their preferred habitat.

(8) On dropping down into the valley, cross a small stream exiting from the wet heath on your right and then begin the rise up onto the lower slopes of Croaghaun, until you reach a cliffed crevice or cove further ahead.

As you descend there are spectacular views of the mighty cliffs on the coastal side of Croaghaun Mountain, dropping as they do from the very apex at 688m. These are some of the highest cliffs in Europe. The worn and tattered cliffs give a good indication of the violent, erosive nature of the sea and should act as a sobering point for anyone that may naively think that these wild cliffs are not prone to collapse.

(9) On reaching the deeply incised, cliffed cove, turn to the RIGHT and follow a straight line above the cove, but keeping well back from the precarious cliffs.

Looking at the rugged rocks of Croaghaun Mountain, you are looking at the end result of 600 million years of geological history.

Comprised primarily of Quartzite, they are essentially some of the oldest in Ireland. During the last glaciation of Ireland they projected above the ice sheets as 'nunatacks' and thus still retain their cliffed ruggedness. While lower mountain peaks were shorn down and rounded as the glaciers moved over them.

(10) On reaching the end of the cliffed cove maintain a STRAIGHT line route, back towards the start of the walk, which is parallel to the cliffed outward journey, now across the valley on your right.

As you proceed, keep well up from the small stream with its associated two small ponds that are visible down on your right, as this area is extremely wet underfoot and makes for uncomfortable walking.

Looking down towards the stream you may spot some stone ruins. These are the remains of an old 'booley village' or summer residence of upland farmers that kept sheep and cattle up here during the dryer summer months.

(11) As you approach the end of the walk, the heath drops sharply downwards with spectacular views out over Keem Bay.

Eventually you approach some old stone ruins, near which an exit track will lead you out passed the abandoned coastguard station and presently onto the tarred road and back down to the car park at the walk's start.

The stone ruins were built by the infamous Captain Charles Boycott, a landlord of the latter part of the nineteenth century. Hated and despised by the people, the building was burnt to the ground and he eventually moved to Ballinrobe, where, because of his treatment of tenants, he was shunned by all and as a consequence his name 'boycott' became part of the English language (*see* Walk 11, Lough Nadirkmore).

BIBLIOGRAPHY

Bence-Jones, Mark, *Burke's Guide to Country Houses*, Vol. 1 Ireland (London 1976).

Brunn, B., Delin, H., Svensson, L., *Birds of Britain and Europe* (Twickenham 1970).

Chinery, Michael, *Field Guide to the Insects of Britain & Northern Europe* (London 1972).

Cunningham, G., *Burren Journey North* (Ballyvaughan 1992).

Herman, D., *Great Walks Ireland* (London 1991).

Kilroy, P., *The Story of Connemara* (Dublin 1989).

Lynam, J., May, J., Robinson, T.D., *The Mountains of Connemara, A Hill-Walker's Guide* (Roundstone 1988).

Martin, W. Keble, *The Concise British Flora in Colour* (London 1965).

Mills, Stephen, *Nature in its Place* (London 1987).

Morris, Pat, *Natural History of the British Isles* (London 1979).

Philips, Rodger, *Grasses, Ferns, Mosses & Lichens of Great Britain and Ireland* (London 1980).

Praeger, R.L., *The Botanist in Ireland* (Dublin 1934).

Robinson, Tim, *Connemara, Part 1, Introduction and Gazetteer* (Roundstone 1990); *Connemara, Part 2, A One-Inch Map* (Roundstone 1990); *The Burren, A Map of the Uplands of North-west Clare* (Roundstone 1977); *The Aran islands, A Map and Guide* (Cill Rónáin 1980).

Scannell, M.J.P., & Synnott D.M., *Census Catalogue of the Flora of Ireland* (Dublin 1987).

Webb, D.A., *An Irish Flora* (Dundalk 1977).

Whilde, T., & Simms, P., *New Irish Walk Guides, West and North* (Dublin 1990).

OTHER WALKING GUIDES
FROM
THE O'BRIEN PRESS

KERRY WALKS
Kevin Corcoran

Twenty walks spread throughout the beautiful and varied countryside of County Kerry, illustrated by the author. The text is also accompanied by detailed location maps, outlining each walk.

WEST CORK WALKS
Kevin Corcoran

Walking in West Cork offers an incredible choice – mountain peaks, rolling heaths, forested valleys, pristine lakes and sandy beaches. Beautifully illustrated by the author, this book covers ten walks, complete with location maps and wildlife illustrations, in superb West Cork.

THE MOURNES WALKS
Paddy Dillon

Thirty-two walks explore the Mournes, taking in rugged coast, high mountains, forest parks and low-level farmlands. The routes lie within the Mourne Area of Outstanding Natural Beauty, and include Slieve Croob and the north-east coastline.

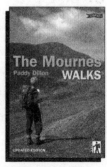

OTHER BOOKS FROM O'BRIEN PRESS

AROUND IRELAND ON A BIKE
Paul Benjaminse
Everything you will need for the perfect cycling holiday: detailed maps, accommodation, travel advice and all you need to know for an unforgettable trip. Taking a route from Belfast to Dublin through the most spectacular scenery and routes that Ireland has to offer.

THE SKELLIG STORY
Des Lavelle
The past, present and future, as well as plant, animal and sea life of Skellig Michael and Small Skellig, two unique historic islands off the southwest coast of Ireland.

THE GOLDEN BOOK OF IRELAND
A beautiful full-colour guide to the whole of Ireland, available in English, German, French, Spanish, Italian and Polish.